China in Malaysia

Edmund Terence Gomez · Siew Yean Tham ·
Ran Li · Kee Cheok Cheong

China in Malaysia

State-Business Relations and the New Order
of Investment Flows

Edmund Terence Gomez
Faculty of Economics and Administration
University of Malaya
Kuala Lumpur, Malaysia

Ran Li
Institute of China Studies
University of Malaya
Kuala Lumpur, Malaysia

Siew Yean Tham
Regional Economic Studies
ISEAS-Yusof Ishak Institute
Singapore, Singapore

Kee Cheok Cheong
Asia-Europe Institute
University of Malaya
Kuala Lumpur, Malaysia

The print edition is not for sale in Malaysia and Singapore. Customers from Malaysia and Singapore please order the print book from: GB Gerakbudaya Enterprise Sdn Bhd. [978-967-2464-10-5].

ISBN 978-981-15-5332-5   ISBN 978-981-15-5333-2 (eBook)
https://doi.org/10.1007/978-981-15-5333-2

© The Editor(s) (if applicable) and The Author(s), under exclusive license to Springer Nature Singapore Pte Ltd. 2020

This work is subject to copyright. All rights are solely and exclusively licensed by the Publisher, whether the whole or part of the material is concerned, specifically the rights of translation, reprinting, reuse of illustrations, recitation, broadcasting, reproduction on microfilms or in any other physical way, and transmission or information storage and retrieval, electronic adaptation, computer software, or by similar or dissimilar methodology now known or hereafter developed.

The use of general descriptive names, registered names, trademarks, service marks, etc. in this publication does not imply, even in the absence of a specific statement, that such names are exempt from the relevant protective laws and regulations and therefore free for general use.

The publisher, the authors and the editors are safe to assume that the advice and information in this book are believed to be true and accurate at the date of publication. Neither the publisher nor the authors or the editors give a warranty, express or implied, with respect to the material contained herein or for any errors or omissions that may have been made. The publisher remains neutral with regard to jurisdictional claims in published maps and institutional affiliations.

Cover image: © Sean Pavone/Alamy Stock Photo

This Palgrave Macmillan imprint is published by the registered company Springer Nature Singapore Pte Ltd.
The registered company address is: 152 Beach Road, #21-01/04 Gateway East, Singapore 189721, Singapore

Preface and Acknowledgments

After President Xi Jinping announced his flagship Belt and Road Initiative (BRI) in 2013, a significant increase in investments flowed from China into Southeast Asia. China's foreign direct investments flows into Malaysia were particularly noteworthy given the close ties that were subsequently forged between Xi and the then prime minister, Najib Razak. China's investments in Malaysia's infrastructure projects as well as in numerous other sectors grew appreciably from 2015. However, as in other countries, media attention and academic research in Malaysia have focussed on the mega infrastructure projects, a number of them controversial in nature, with much discussion about potential debt-traps and the limited transparency surrounding the award of these contracts.

Meanwhile, very little attention has been paid to investments in the industrial sector, even after a significant inflow of such funds from China into Malaysia, as well as other Southeast Asian countries. This served as the reason for our decision to assess what was occurring in this sector, after we started discussing our respective work on BRI-based projects. Many intriguing points emerged during our discussions, prompting us to delve further into this lacuna in the research on the BRI. An initial typology of the different projects in the industrial sector convinced us of the need for a new framework. Although there are three economists among us, it was unanimously agreed that a purely economic framework was not suitable as it cannot explain the varied nature of these investments, the complexity of the transactions and the different outcomes in each project. Indeed, a careful assessment was required of the stakeholders involved in these projects. Hours of intense discussions eventually paved the way for a new approach towards the framing of our analysis for this monograph, leading to a unique perspective as well as fresh insights about the nature of China's investments in the industrial sector.

The sheer heterogeneity of investors and outcomes in the different projects indicated to us the need to employ a case study approach to examine the diverse features of these investments. The selection of the cases was based on the classification of the projects, to ensure each category was covered in our study. Since the BRI projects are rather new, with most of them less than five years old at the time of our research, we had to use a combination of methods to extract the data for our analysis, including primary (interviews) and secondary sources. This was not the easiest of tasks as firm-level data from the Department of Statistics (DOS), Malaysia, is not available due to the Statistics Act, which keeps confidential the information obtained from individual respondents. This information cannot be disclosed to any third party. There is also a three to two-year time-lag between DOS's surveys and published data. This meant that aggregated data would probably not capture some of the relatively new investments. The directors and senior managers of these companies were not always keen to be interviewed because of the many controversies surrounding China's foreign investments. We have, however, attempted, to the best of our abilities, to capture the perspectives of investors from Malaysia and China when assessing these cases, creating a balance in the views of the host and investing countries.

The projects were assessed based on their stated objectives, as well as their long-term developmental implications. The latter was necessary as foreign direct investments, including inflows from China, are courted for their potential contribution to a host country's economic growth and, particularly in the case of Malaysia, the development of domestic enterprises, primarily small- and medium-scale enterprises through the creation of supply chains. This is particularly important when investment projects are costly and will be in the host economy over a protracted period. Malaysia's dilemma in moving towards a higher stage of industrialisation is well covered in academic and public policy debates. As such, this assessment of the long-term objectives of China's ventures in Malaysia provides invaluable lessons for managing these investments, not just for this country but for other emerging economies.

Although the process of writing this slim volume was shorter than usual, the journey was exceptionally rich and fruitful for us as we learnt to untangle the evolution of each investment, based on our many conversations. As in all joint writing endeavours, it is the researchers who are enriched through knowledge-sharing and we hope that this will be the case for the readers as well.

The funding for this study was obtained from the Competing Regional Integrations in Southeast Asia (CRISEA) project, supported by the European Union's Horizon 2020 Framework Programme. We acknowledge with gratitude the support of the CRISEA management for this project, in particular, Jacques Leider and Elisabeth Lacroix. We are deeply indebted to Lau Zheng Zhou and the team of young research assistants he assembled to gather the data reviewed in this study. When we began this project, we were constantly told that it would be difficult to obtain information about the companies from China that had invested in Malaysia. This team of young researchers worked diligently to collect the information we required. Lengthy discussions were held with them to determine how to classify and present the data that had been obtained. We thank this team of young researchers for the time they devoted to compiling this database and we hope they benefited from this research exercise.

We thank the ISEAS-Yusof Ishak Institute in Singapore for encouraging research involving BRI projects. The discussions during the numerous seminars on the BRI at ISEAS served as a venue where we obtained useful insights for this study. We thank members of the Ministry of International Trade and Industry, IJM Corporation, Malaysia Airport Holdings Bhd and Alliance Steel for the interviews we had with them. We further acknowledge, and with much gratitude, Ban Yandong, from Sino Trade Crest Sdn Bhd, and Zhai Yibo, from the Embassy of the People's Republic of China in Malaysia, who helped us contact Chinese companies for interviews and arranged site visits. We thank those we interviewed when we visited these Chinese companies for they generously provided the information we required for this study. We appreciate that Associate Professor Dr. Kuik Cheng Chwee from the Institute of Malaysian and International Studies, Universiti Kebangsaan Malaysia shared his research findings with us. We acknowledge the support of the director of Institute of China Studies, University of Malaya, Dr. Ngeow Chow Bing. We are deeply indebted to Palgrave Macmillan's Vishal Daryanomel for arranging the review of the manuscript—indeed, even the extremely useful feedback we obtained was sent to us very quickly—and for his tireless efforts in making this research project possible as a monograph.

While we are indebted to those mentioned here for their kind support to our research, we, the authors, remain solely responsible for the contents of this book.

March 2020

Edmund Terence Gomez
Siew Yean Tham
Ran Li
Kee Cheok Cheong

The original version of the book was inadvertently published without information regarding copyright, which has now been incorporated. The book has been updated with the changes.

Contents

1 Introduction: State-State Relations and New
  State-Business Relations—China in Malaysia ... 1

2 State-Business Relations—Multinational SOEs, GLCs,
  and SMEs ... 15

3 Chinese Investment Case Studies from Malaysia ... 25

4 Analysing Chinese Investments in Malaysia ... 75

5 Conclusion ... 97

Appendix 1: Investments by Firms from China in Malaysia ... 105

Bibliography ... 113

About the Authors

Edmund Terence Gomez is Professor of Political Economy at the Faculty of Economics and Administration, University of Malaya. His publications include *Malaysia's Political Economy: Politics, Patronage and Profits* (Cambridge University Press, 1997), *Chinese Business in Malaysia: Accumulation, Ascendance, Accommodation* (University of Hawaii Press, 1999), *Political Business in East Asia* (Routledge, 2002), *Government-Linked Companies and Sustainable, Equitable Development* (Routledge, 2014) and *Minister of Finance Incorporated: Ownership and Control of Corporate Malaysia* (Palgrave Macmillan, 2017).

Siew Yean Tham is Visiting Senior Fellow at ISEAS-Yusof Ishak, Singapore and Professor Emeritus, Universiti Kebangsaan Malaysia. She was formerly Director and Professor of International Trade at the Institute of Malaysian and International Studies (IKMAS), Universiti Kebangsaan Malaysia. Her research interests cover trade in goods and services as well as foreign direct investment (FDI). She has published extensively on trade-related issues in journals such as *Journal of Contemporary Asia, Emerging Markets, Finance and Trade, Asian Economic Panel* and *Prague Economic Papers*, besides co-editing several books published by international publishing houses.

Ran Li is Senior Lecturer at Institute of China Studies, University of Malaya. She obtained her doctoral degree in Economics from University of Malaya in 2014. Her specialisation is in the transformation of China's state enterprises and China's political-economic system. Her areas of research include China's global strategy and China–Malaysia economic relations. Her writings have appeared in a number of international journals such as *China: An International Journal*, *Cities*, *International Journal of China Studies* and *Journal of Contemporary Asia*. Her doctoral thesis was published as a book by Palgrave Macmillan in 2019.

Kee Cheok Cheong is Senior Advisor, Asia-Europe Institute, University of Malaya. A graduate of the University of Malaya, he obtained his Ph.D. at the London School of Economics. He has held the positions of Dean at the Faculty of Economics and Administration, University of Malaya, and senior economist at the World Bank, Washington D.C., for which he continues to consult after he left. Since his return to Malaysia, he has co-authored a number of books, book chapters and over 40 papers in academic journals. His research interests include economic development, transition economies, particularly China and Vietnam, international economic relations, education and human capital and economic history, specifically relating to the Chinese overseas.

Abbreviations

1MDB	1Malaysia Development Bhd
ACA	Automation Capital Allowance
AFTA	ASEAN Free Trade Agreement
AIIB	Asia Infrastructure Investment Bank
ASZ1	Aeronautical Support Zone 1
B2B	Business-to-Business
B2C	Business-to-Consumer
BRI	Belt and Road Initiative
CCB	China Construction Bank
CCCC	China Communication Construction Co. Ltd.
CCM	Companies Commission of Malaysia
CEO	Chief Executive Officer
CFO	Chief Financial Officer
CGBGIP	China Guangxi Beibu Gulf International Port Group
CKD	Completely-Knocked-Down
CMQIP	China-Malaysia Qinzhou Industrial Park
CNTAC	China National Textile and Apparel Council
CRRC	CRRC Corporation Ltd
CRRC CRM	CRRC Rolling Stock Center (Malaysia) Sdn Bhd
CRRC ZELC	CRRC Zhuzhou Locomotive Co. Ltd.
CTO	Chief Technical Officer
DFTZ	Digital Free Trade Zone
DMU	Diesel Multiple Unit
DSI	Drivetrain Systems International
ECER	East Coast Economic Region
ECERDC	East Coast Economic Region Development Council

ECRL	East Coast Rail Link
EMU	Electric Multiple Unit
EPU	Economic Planning Unit
ETP	Economic Transformation Programme
e-WTP	Electronic-World Trade Platform
FDI	Foreign Direct Investment
fwt	Freight Weight Tonnes
GBG	Guangxi Beibu Gulf Port International Group Co. Ltd.
GDP	Gross Domestic Product
GLCs	Government-Linked Companies
GSM	Guangxi Shenglong Metallugical
HICOM	Heavy Industries Corporation of Malaysia Bhd
HKTDC	Hong Kong Trade Development Council
HST	High Speed Train
IFC	International Finance Corporation
IR4.0	Industrial Revolution 4.0
ISGA	Turkey's Sabiha Gokcen International
JCC	Joint Cooperation Council
KLIA	Kuala Lumpur International Airport
KPI	Key Performance Indicator
KTMB	Keretapi Tanah Melayu Bhd
LCCT	Low-Cost Carrier Terminal
LRT3	Light Rail Transit Line 3
LRV	Light Rail Vehicle
M&As	Mergers and Acquisitions
MAHB	Malaysia Airports Holdings Bhd
MARii	Malaysia Automotive Robotics and IoT Institute
MCKIP	Malaysia-China Kuantan Industrial Park
MICE	Meetings, Incentives, Conferences and Exhibitions
MIDA	Malaysian Investment Development Authority
MITI	Ministry of International Trade and Industry
MNCs	Multinational Companies
MRL	Malaysia Rail Link Sdn Bhd
MRT	Mass Rapid Transit
NCER	Northern Corridor Economic Region
NDB	New Development Bank
NTU	Nanyang Technology University
PERC	Passivated Emitter Rear Cells
PONSB	Perusahaan Otomobil Nasional Sdn Bhd
PPPs	Public-Private Partnerships
PV	Photovoltaics
QJIC	Qinzhou Jinqu Investment Company Ltd
R&D	Research and Development

REIT	Real Estate Investment Trust
RHD	Right-Hand Drive
SASAC	State-Owned Assets Supervision and Administration Commission of the State Council
SBRs	State-Business Relations
SCO	Shanghai Cooperation Organisation
SCORE	Sarawak Corridor of Renewable Energy
SDC	Sabah Development Corridor
Sinopec	China Petroleum and Chemical Corporation
SMEs	Small- and Medium-Scale Enterprises
SOEs	State-Owned Enterprises
SUV	Sports Utility Vehicle
TDA	Technology Depository Agency
TPP	Trans-Pacific Partnership
UOB	United Overseas Bank
VDP	Vendor Development Programme
VP	Vice President

LIST OF FIGURES

Fig. 1.1	FDI Net Inflows, 2010–2019 (RM million) (*Source* Compiled from *Statistics on Foreign Direct Investment in Malaysia*, Department of Statistics, Malaysia, [various years])	7
Fig. 1.2	China-Related Projects in Malaysia (*Source* Extracted from Appendix 1)	9
Fig. 1.3	China in Malaysia: Different forms of State-Business Relations (*Source* Based on Appendix 1)	11
Fig. 1.4	Approved Investments in Manufacturing, 2010–2018 (*Source* Malaysian Investment Development Authority [MIDA], unpublished data)	14

List of Tables

Table 1.1	China's Importance in the Trade of Southeast Asian Countries, 2017	3
Table 1.2	Patterns of Chinese Greenfield Investments in BRI-Linked Areas, 2015 (in US$ millions)	5
Table 1.3	China in Malaysia: Different forms of State-Business Relations	13
Table 4.1	Summary of the seven cases	76

CHAPTER 1

Introduction: State-State Relations and New State-Business Relations—China in Malaysia

THE CONTEXT

In September 2013, when President Xi Jinping announced China's intent to implement its Belt-Road Initiative (BRI),[1] its breadth and scope promptly spawned an extensive debate about its actual objectives. The BRI's often-cited objective is that this plan serves as a mechanism for China to secure access to the energy and resources of countries in emerging economies in Southeast Asia, Central Asia and Europe. What's more, the BRI professedly serves to cultivate a network of economic interdependence involving inter-linked countries in these continents, a method that, presumably, would help to maintain regional stability. The BRI's official objectives are five-fold: policy coordination, connecting infrastructure, unimpeded trade, financial integration and people-to-people bonds. Beyond these specific objectives are broader perspectives of China's desire to re-make a world order that it feels is heavily biased in favour of the West (Chatsky and McBride 2019; Macaes 2019). There is a history and logic to these narratives.

In 2001, with China's sponsorship, the Shanghai Cooperation Organisation (SCO) was established. The constituent members of the SCO were

---

[1] For a comprehensive historical review of the BRI, since its inception, see Chang (2019). See also Frankopan's (2018) account of the 'new silk roads' for a broader history of China's inter-connectedness with emerging economies. Miller (2017) provides a more contemporary review of China's entry into emerging economies through the BRI.

© The Author(s) 2020
E. T. Gomez et al., *China in Malaysia*,
https://doi.org/10.1007/978-981-15-5333-2_1

China, Kazakhstan, Kyrgyzstan, Russia, Tajikistan and Uzbekistan.[2] India and Pakistan joined the SCO in 2017. There are considerable similarities in the objectives and roles of the SCO and BRI. For instance, the official BRI goals are similarly espoused by the SCO. There are overlaps in their economic domains. And, the SCO's principal objective is economic integration of the entire Asian continent (Rowden 2018; Cai 2017). In October 2012, Wang (2012), at Peking University, proposed that China rebalance its geopolitical strategy towards Central Asia and Eurasia.[3] The BRI would go on to expand this coverage to include nations of the Indian and Pacific Oceans. The BRI combines two initiatives—the (land-based) Silk Road Economic Belt, comprising six development corridors, and the 21st-Century Maritime Silk Road.[4]

Another aspect of the BRI, one related to its execution was the launch of the Asia Infrastructure Investment Bank (AIIB) and the New Development Bank (NDB), both in 2015.[5] By 2017, China had become a key stakeholder in Southeast Asia's economic development, being the top trading partner of more than half the countries of Southeast Asia (Table 1.1). There has also been a surge in investments by China into Southeast Asia.

Based on a review of China's investments in Southeast Asia, this volume argues, with case studies of specific enterprises as evidence, that an important outcome of the BRI is that of growing 'state-state' ties.[6] These

---

[2] The SCO, an extension of the Shanghai Five, founded in 1996, now included Uzbekistan.

[3] See also Lim (2015).

[4] What constitutes the BRI for this study is as stated in its official website: https://www.beltroad-initiative.com/belt-and-road. The BRI website also draws reference to the Polar Silk Road that embodies China's Artic Policy. This website also provides a list of BRI projects.

[5] The AIIB's articles of agreement entered into force on 25 December 2015 and the bank opened for business on 16 January 2016. As of January 2019, the AIIB has 74 members and is headquartered in Beijing https://www.aiib.org/en/about-aiib/governance/members-of-bank/index.html. The NDB, originally called the BRICS Development Bank, was proposed by India at the 4th BRICS Summit in 2012. In July 2015, at the 7th BRICS Summit, the Agreement of the NDB came into force. The NDB's members are the five BRIC countries, with the bank headquartered in Shanghai.

[6] For example, one Chinese SOE, China Railway No. 3 Engineering Group Co. Ltd, has cooperated with the Ministry of State-Owned Enterprises of Indonesia on

Table 1.1 China's Importance in the Trade of Southeast Asian Countries, 2017

Country	China's Rank as Export Destination	China's Rank as Import Source	China's Rank as Trading Partner[a]
Brunei	>5	1	4
Cambodia	>5	1	1
Indonesia	1	1	1
Laos	1	2	2
Malaysia	2	1	1
Myanmar	1	1	1
Philippines	4	1	1
Singapore	1	1	1
Thailand	1	1	1
Vietnam	2	1	1

[a]Trade refers to the sum of exports and imports
Source Cheong and Yong (2019: 20)

state-state ties forged by China with Southeast Asian countries are particularly visible in Malaysia. Based on these state-state ties, enterprises owned by the governments of both countries have been employed to jointly mount projects, creating what can be classified as 'public-public partnerships'. However, private investors are still privy to government incentives. In the process, novel and diverse forms of 'state-business relations' have emerged, with some ventures controversial in nature, with evidence of anomalies, while others have potentially productive outcomes.

THE STATE'S CENTRAL ROLE

This book focuses on the implications of two core and related issues: first, the central role of the state in economic development in Southeast Asia. Second, the active role of the Chinese state in business, through its state-owned enterprises (SOEs),[7] has contributed to the building of a new state-business order, one fundamentally different from the dominant neoliberal system created by the United States and its allies after the Second World War.

the Jakarta-Bandung high-speed rail project, see: https://www.straitstimes.com/asia/se-asia/jakarta-bandung-high-speed-rail-project-back-on-track-says-indonesias-investment-chief and http://www.xinhuanet.com/world/2019-05/14/c_1124494049.htm.

[7] For an in-depth review of China's SOEs, see Li and Cheong (2019).

On the first issue, a lack of democratic tradition among diverse political systems and widely reported rising authoritarianism are factors that have contributed to a strong state in Southeast Asia.[8] In this book, the centrality of the state in Southeast Asian economies is reviewed through an assessment of business links fashioned by the governments of China and Malaysia, a nexus that has contributed to an escalation of the phenomenon of state-state relations.[9] The economic relations between China and Malaysia, cultivated through the active deployment of companies owned by these two governments, have fostered the rise of important novel and innovative forms of state-business relations (SBRs), or affiliations between governments and businesses. A different mode of entry by multinational companies into developing economies has emerged, through investments implemented by SOEs and state-supported private enterprises.[10] To ensure the implementation of these projects, the funds have been provided by China's state-owned financial institutions.

Soon after the BRI was introduced, numerous countries in Southeast Asia promptly endorsed this plan as it proposed the creation of major infrastructure and industrial projects in the region, with funding provided by China-based financial institutions. In fact, the number of countries linked to the BRI has increased since 2013, from 64 to 130, and now includes an industrialised G7, Italy (*The Diplomat*, 24 April 2019).[11] However, as Table 1.2 indicates, Southeast Asian countries have benefited most from greenfield-based investments related to the BRI, compared to other regions in Asia and Europe. This is in line with overall inflows of

---

[8] See Barber (2018) and Thompson (2019) for an account of the re-emergence of authoritarian trends in democratised Southeast Asian countries.

[9] For another perspective on the concept of state-state relations involving China, see Singh and Chen (2017).

[10] State-supported private enterprises refer to influential privately-owned companies that are closely linked to elites in power. Such well-connected firms, in which the state has no equity ownership, are privy to significant support through government-generated rents, such as contracts and licences, as well as funds from government-linked financial institutions. State support of this sort is ostensibly a means to 'pick winners' who will play a role in the development of a country. State support is also provided through strategic public policies promulgated to develop core sectors of the economy. Examples of major enterprises in China that have benefited from state support are Huawei and Alibaba.

[11] See also: https://thediplomat.com/2019/04/china-italy-relations-the-bri-effect/. However, according to the official BRI website, by early 2020, there were 118 BRI-based projects. These differing figures indicate that there are diverse viewpoints among people in the media, academia and government about what constitutes a BRI project.

Table 1.2 Patterns of Chinese Greenfield Investments in BRI-Linked Areas, 2015 (in US$ millions)

Sectors	ASEAN	South Asia	West Asia	CIS[a]	Central and Eastern Europe	Central Asia	Total
Manufacturing	436.5	164.8	165.5	156.7	75.4	46.9	1064.8
Electricity	129.6	175.7	20.1	11.5	12.9	8.9	358.7
Mining	55.3	35.4	79.3	5.1	0.0	16.0	196.0
Construction	55.7	8.7	3.9	28.4	3.8	0.8	103.6
Logistics	33.8	5.6	3.5	2.0	4.4	26.9	76.4

Note [a]Commonwealth of Independent States
Source FDI Intelligence Database (https://www.fdiintelligence.com/)

foreign direct investments (FDI) into Asia, with most of them entering the economies of East and Southeast Asia. This is because these countries, particularly China and ASEAN, are more open to FDI, compared to other countries in the region. To implement these mutually beneficial economic ties, fostered through active state-state relations, multi-national SOEs from China have created joint-ventures with government-owned as well as private enterprises in Southeast Asia.

Another factor shaping the construction of new forms of SBRs is that of the political system of a country. Southeast Asia is interesting as countries in this region are characterised by different political systems, the products of their respective histories since the Second World War. Cambodia and Singapore–Malaysia too, before May 2018–are governed by hegemonic single dominant parties. Laos and Vietnam have one-party communist systems. Brunei is under monarchical rule, while Thailand, after a period of military rule is now a democracy though governed by leaders of the previous military regime. Indonesia, the Philippines and Timor-Leste are democratic countries, though they are far from consolidating it, while Myanmar is in transition to a functioning democracy.[12] In most of these countries, characterised by autocratic leadership (Kurlantzick 2018) and extensive state intervention, state-state relations

---

[12] For an in-depth discussion on the political systems in Southeast Asia, see McCarthy and Thompson (2019).

have facilitated investment flows from China for BRI-based projects to be implemented by Chinese SOEs.

On the second core issue, the economic dominance of the Chinese state can be explained by the history of the People's Republic (PRC). Since its establishment, the PRC had adopted a system of central planning in which all economic decisions were made by the state; the private sector did not exist. The private sector emerged from two milestones in China's economic transformation. The first was President Deng Xiaoping's economic liberalisation which entailed the introduction of market principles in economic transactions, the so-called 'contract responsibility system' (Koo 1990). The second was a series of state enterprise reforms, particularly those initiated in the early 1990s by then Premier Zhu Rongji. This led to the restructuring of a large number SOEs that were privatised or closed (Li and Cheong 2019). Indeed, most private enterprises in China began life as SOEs. These private firms now have—or have had—close ties with SOEs, while also adhering faithfully to economic strategies promulgated by the state. In that sense then, the separation between the Chinese state and private enterprises is nowhere as sharp as in a market economy, as this study will also show.

Table 1.2 further highlights the stress on manufacturing, in terms of the total value of the investments. Investments in manufacturing are frequently in the form of FDI. Meanwhile, the mode of financing of investments in other sectors, especially in the case of infrastructure, such as electricity projects as in the case of hydro-power, tends to be in the form of loans. Logistics investments, evidenced in the case of Alibaba's activities in Southeast Asia, are undertaken through mergers and acquisitions (M&As), rather than greenfield investments.

Malaysia is a fascinating case study as it was quick to endorse the BRI, in order to tap into the investment funds that would flow in from China.[13] Malaysia was particularly keen in 2013 to identify new sources of FDI as such fund flows served as an important mechanism to offset

---

[13] Malaysia was the first ASEAN country to establish diplomatic relations with China in 1974. But economic exchanges between the two territories, in the form of migration and remittances, preceded these diplomatic relations by about two centuries. But relations between the two countries were disrupted when the PRC was established in 1949, and not normalized until the premiership of Mahathir Mohamad in about 1990.

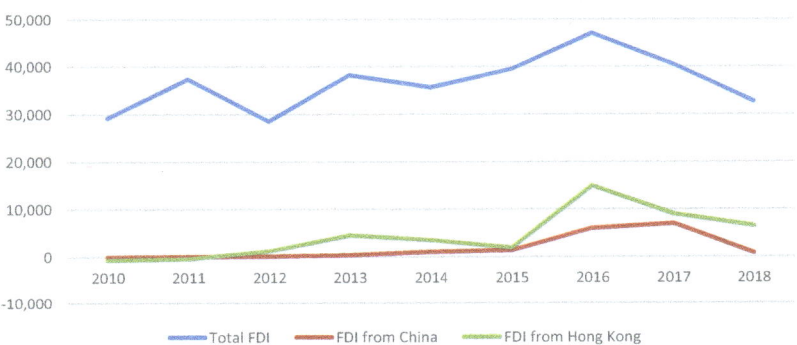

Fig. 1.1 FDI Net Inflows, 2010–2019 (RM million) (*Source* Compiled from *Statistics on Foreign Direct Investment in Malaysia*, Department of Statistics, Malaysia, [various years])

declining domestic investments.[14] As Fig. 1.1 indicates, a surge in investments into Malaysia from China occurred after 2013, particularly after then Prime Minister Najib Razak signed 14 memoranda of understanding with Chinese companies for economic cooperation. Although the share of FDI from China to Malaysia is relatively small to the total, investments were also channelled through Hong Kong.[15] FDI from Hong Kong had also increased over time, especially after 2015. The slow-down observed in 2017 and 2018 can be attributed to the general deterioration in Malaysia's investment climate, due possibly to the exposé of the 1MDB

---

[14] One reason for this decline in domestic investments was the outcome of the general election in 2013, when the then ruling coalition, the *Barisan Nasional* (National Front), fared badly. In response, the government introduced an ethnically-based discriminatory policy to muster political support from Malays, Malaysia's majority ethnic group. However, this policy, based on, among other things, affirmative action in business, undermined domestic investor confidence. For an in-depth analysis of this issue and the implications of the introduction of this race-based policy which eventually contributed to the fall of the Barisan Nasional in the May 2018 general election, see Gomez and Mohamed Nawab (2020).

[15] Investments by privately-owned companies from China into Malaysia through Hong Kong will be indicated in the case studies of Geely, which acquired an interest in Proton, the national car, and Cainiao's venture in the digital free trade zone (DFTZ).

scandal in 2015,[16] while regional competitors such as Vietnam have progressively improved their economies by reforming their investment laws.[17]

These funds from China were also channelled to implement numerous major infrastructure and construction-based projects around Malaysia, with the largest ones indicated in Fig. 1.2. Not long later, after the approval of a number of these projects, President Xi described China's relationship with Malaysia as 'being at its best'.[18] These infrastructure and construction-based projects have received an inordinate volume of media attention because a number of them have been mired in controversy.

The most controversial of these projects was the East Coast Rail Link (ECRL), one that constituted a major segment of China's BRI. This project entailed the construction of a 688 km railway line between the industrialised state of Selangor, on the west coast of the peninsula, and the under-developed eastern states of Pahang, Terengganu and Kelantan. In November 2016, Malaysia Rail Link Sdn Bhd (MRL), an enterprise owned by the Malaysian government, entered into a contract valued at RM55 billion with a leading Chinese SOE, China Communication Construction Co. Ltd. (CCCC). A loan, amounting to 85% of the contract value, was secured from a finance-based SOE, the Export-Import Bank of China, to implement the project, to be repaid over 20 years. The Malaysian government justified the acceptance of this huge loan on the grounds that it was given at a favourable interest rate and that the project

---

[16] In 2015, the misappropriation of funds from a public enterprise, 1Malaysia Development Bhd (1MDB) was exposed. This scandal linked missing money from 1MDB to the deposit of RM2.6 billion (approximately US$700 million in 2015) into the personal bank account of Prime Minister Najib. The funds from this account were allegedly used during the 2013 general election. For a detailed account of the 1MDB scandal, see Wright and Hope (2018).

[17] Media statement by Ong Kian Ming, then Deputy Minister of the Ministry of International Trade and Industry (MITI), on 10 January 2019, "How much more Foreign Direct Investment (FDI) would Malaysia have attracted without Najib and the scandal of 1MDB hanging over the heads of foreign investors?" https://ongkianming.com/2019/01/10/media-statement-how-much-more-foreign-direct-investment-fdi-would-malaysia-have-attracted-without-najib-and-the-scandal-of-1mdb-hanging-over-the-heads-of-foreign-investors/.

[18] Rachel Lau, "China's Belt and Road: What's in it for Malaysia?" *Borneo Post*, 3 September 2017. http://www.theborneopost.com/2017/09/03/chinas-belt-and-road-whats-in-it-for-malaysia/.

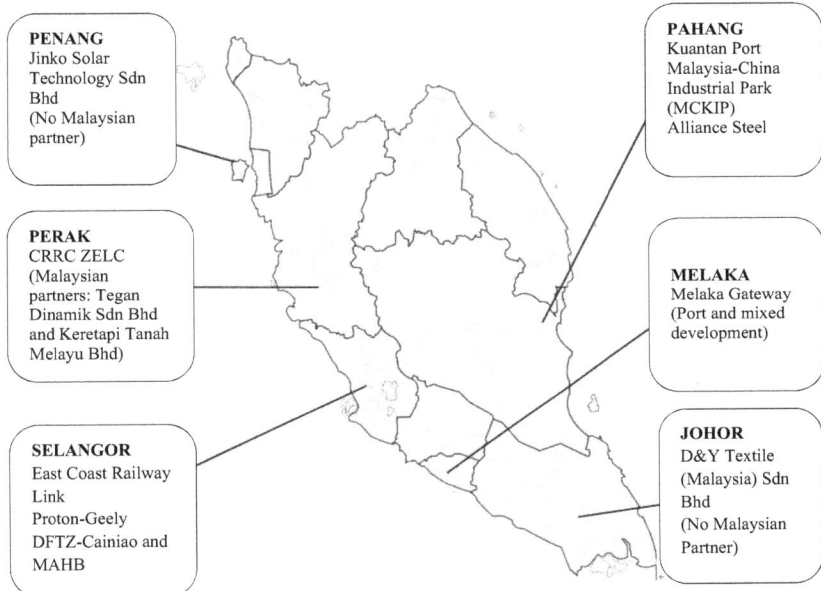

Fig. 1.2 China-Related Projects in Malaysia (*Source* Extracted from Appendix 1)

would help fulfil its longstanding objective of industrialising the underdeveloped eastern states in the peninsula.[19] However, the ECRL project was reportedly extremely over-valued, with allegations that funds from this loan were channelled to 1MDB to resolve its debt crisis (see Wright and Hope 2018).

A large number of the projects listed in Fig. 1.2, emerging from investments from China, were implemented by its multinational SOEs, in collaboration with government-linked companies (GLCs) from Malaysia;

---

[19] For in-depth reports about the controversy surrounding the ECRL project, see: http://www.theedgemarkets.com/article/world%E2%80%99s-costliest-railway; https://www.edgeprop.my/content/962916/ecrl-not-world%E2%80%99s-costliest-rail-project; http://www.theedgemarkets.com/article/rafizi-ecrl-deal-signed-rm2-company-formed-without-parliaments-approval; and https://www.edgeprop.my/content/954096/release-ecrl-feasibility-study-say-opposition-mps.

in some cases, privately-owned firms were included in these joint-ventures. However, what has not been adequately noted is that SOEs, as well as privately-owned companies, from China had also begun actively investing in Malaysia in projects that were not necessarily BRI-linked, reinforcing the view that this plan was inaugurated to support China's longstanding 'going out' strategy,[20] introduced in 1999.[21] These Chinese private firms in Malaysia have a marked presence in the industrial and manufacturing sectors; in some cases, joint-ventures were created between them and Malaysian companies. State-state relations between China and Malaysia had demonstrably opened avenues for private firms from both countries to venture into business areas that can contribute to productive economic outcomes, including generating employment and creating new products and services.

An in-depth study of China's investments in Malaysia uncovered 92 SOEs and private firms operating in this Southeast Asian country.[22] These 92 enterprises were involved in a diverse range of sectors. When implementing these projects, these Chinese enterprises had created different sorts of SBRs that can be classified as 'state-state', 'state-state-private', 'state-private' and 'state-private-private' (see Fig. 1.3). In some cases, private firms from China and Malaysia had forged 'private-private' ties, through joint-ventures. In other projects, private enterprises, as well as SOEs, from China ran projects without the participation of Malaysian companies. It should be noted that a number of these private enterprises from China originated from the state sector. A large number of them

---

[20] When the Chinese government introduced its 'going out' strategy in 1999, it was described as an endeavour to, among other things, develop export trade and speed up 'adjustment of industrial structure' as well as to transfer abroad 'mature technology and industry'. This was to be done by 'strong enterprises' that would invest overseas through methods such as 'foreign processing and assembling' and by driving the 'export of domestic equipment, technology, materials and semi-finished products', a means also to 'expand the foreign trade'. These quotes were retrieved from the government's official 'going out' development strategy. For full details, see: http://history.mofcom.gov.cn/?newchina = %E4%B8%AD%E5%9B%BD%E4%BC%81%E4%B8%9A%E8%B5%B0%E5%87%BA %E5%8E%BB%E5%8F%91%E5%B1%95%E6%88%98%E7%95%A5.

[21] For a review of the 'going out' strategy, see Shen and Mantzopoulos (2013) and Li (2018).

[22] Appendix 1 provides a list of these 92 enterprises from China that have invested in the Malaysian economy.

1 INTRODUCTION: STATE-STATE RELATIONS ...   11

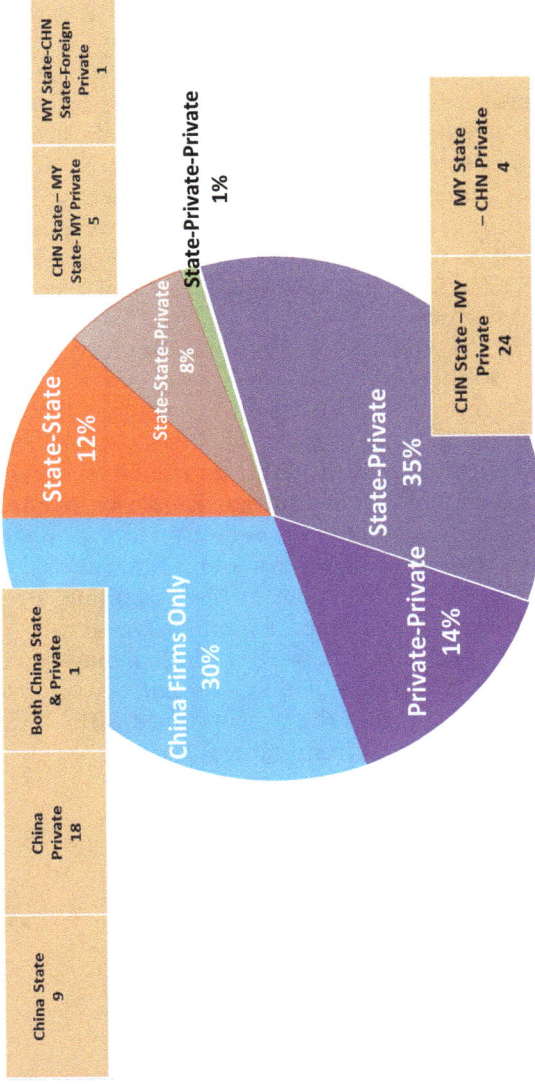

Fig. 1.3 China in Malaysia: Different forms of State-Business Relations (*Source* Based on Appendix 1)

continue to be partially-owned by the government or depend on SOEs as sources of technology.[23]

The reach of the state in China's corporate sector is rather extensive, one that a simple state-private dichotomy does not capture. The enterprises in these different SBRs are involved in the industrial, manufacturing, services, property development and agriculture sectors, though a majority of these investments were channelled to infrastructure and construction-based projects (see Table 1.3). From these diverse SBR forms have emerged different outcomes, some predatory in nature, reflecting elements of rent-seeking. Other projects, however, have been more developmental in nature, resulting in the creation of infrastructure that facilitates trade as well as the incorporation of new industries that foster technological progress.

The case studies in this volume focus on manufacturing and services due to the higher number of projects in these two sub-sectors, as compared to the other sectors (see Table 1.3). The volume of investments in manufacturing has also increased appreciably between 2010 and 2018, as indicated in Fig. 1.4. Moreover, the focus on manufacturing indicates that the sectors that China's SOEs and private firms have invested in are what are seen as priority areas when overseas investments are undertaken. The 'Guideline of the State Council on Promoting International Cooperation in Production Capacity and Equipment Manufacturing' stresses the Chinese government's desire to deepen national development through the BRI, a mechanism also to accelerate its longstanding 'going out' strategy. However, before assessing China's SOEs and private enterprises in Malaysia, a review is required of the newly-formed SBRs, manifested through these investments derived from state-state ties.

---

[23] For a discussion on the emergence of well-connected private companies in China, see Pei (2016).

Table 1.3 China in Malaysia: Different forms of State-Business Relations

Forms of ownership	Industrial/Manufacturing	Services	Construction	Infrastructure	Agriculture	Total by Type
State-State	4	1	2	5	0	12
State-State-Private	3	0	1	2	0	6
State-Private-Private	0	1	0	0	0	1
State-Private	4	1	13	10	0	28
Private-Private	3	2	8	3	1	17
China Firms Only (SOEs & private)	20	1	6	1	0	28
Total by sector	35	6	30	20	1	

Source Based on Appendix 1

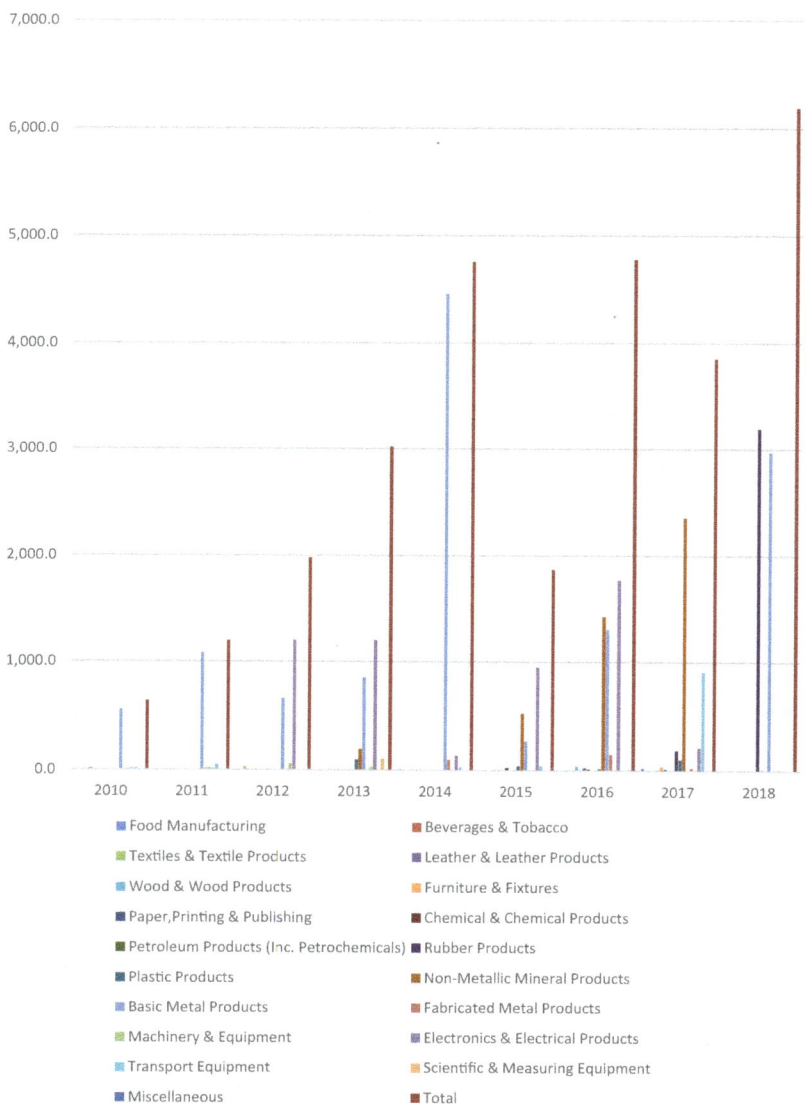

Fig. 1.4 Approved Investments in Manufacturing, 2010–2018 (*Source* Malaysian Investment Development Authority [MIDA], unpublished data)

CHAPTER 2

State-Business Relations—Multinational SOEs, GLCs, and SMEs

Reviewing Emerging State-Business Relations (SBRs)

The conventional understanding of an SBR is that of a nexus between the public and private sectors, widely referred to as public-private partnerships (PPPs). In PPPs, large private firms, usually multinational companies (MNCs), as controllers of capital, can exert much power over governments by deciding if they should invest in publicly-conceived projects. In this literature, through PPPs, powerful private firms, primarily MNCs, can capture control of the state by financing political parties or politicians in power.[1] Inevitably, the focus of scholars of SBRs has been on the way states and businesses interact.[2] The outcomes of SBRs rest heavily on how special interest groups, or lobbies, function and their capacity to frame policies that best serve the interests of their clients, such as big banks, large pharmaceuticals, etc.[3]

The decisions made by MNCs about where to invest are based on several factors, comprising a comparative assessment of resource costs, policies and incentives offered by governments. Indeed, the influence

---

[1] Leonard (1980) provides a comprehensive review of the literature on the funding of politics by MNCs in developing economies.

[2] See, for example, Maxfield and Schneider (1997), Khanna and Yafeh (2007), Fuchs and Lederer (2007), Schneider (2009), and Culpepper (2015).

[3] See, for example, Woll (2008) and Culpepper (2010).

© The Author(s) 2020
E. T. Gomez et al., *China in Malaysia*,
https://doi.org/10.1007/978-981-15-5333-2_2

of MNCs is such that they can invest or threaten exit if their demands are not met. This reflects a form of 'structural power' that allows MNCs to compel governments to promulgate policies that serve their business interests.[4] This structural power, as Weiss and Thurbon (2018) note, draws attention to the capacity of an institution to project power abroad. In SBRs in emerging economies, this structural power is manifested in the ability of MNCs to set the rules of a game in production, investment, knowledge, finance and trade, and in ways that tilt the playing field to their own advantage (Weiss and Thurborn 2018).

Scholars of SBRs also note that large enterprises can influence policy outcomes by financing political campaigns, as well as through the paying of bribes and active lobbying. The practice of 'revolving doors' has also been noted in numerus countries, a situation where businesspeople enter the government in order to have a strong hand in shaping policies.[5] In such contexts, the business actors determine the resources at their command and accordingly act to fulfil their economic interests, though Fuchs and Lederer (2007) acknowledge that even here the situation can be decidedly structural 'based on the agenda-setting power of actors involved'.

Another core concern in debates about PPPs is whether an appropriate 'institutional architecture' is available as this is key to the promulgation of viable policies to draw private investments. Three key elements inform the functionality of an institutional architecture: first, political leadership, with specific focus on the apex of the political system. Second, the existence of deliberation councils, as well as coordination between them. And, finally, the degree of transparency and accountability within the governance system. In this institutional architecture, there is a fourfold key concern: first, transparency, in the flow of accurate and reliable information between the government and business sector. Second, reciprocity, that is the capacity and autonomy of a government to secure viable economic performance from companies in return for subsidies or other forms of public support. Third, credibility, i.e. if the government

---

[4] Farrell and Newman (2015) provide a thoughtful discussion on the structural power of MNCs. See also Culpepper (2015).

[5] For an in-depth discussion of these issues, see Holcombe (2018).

commands it and if businesses accept as true what politicians and bureaucrats say. Fourth, mutual trust between the government and business, in all the preceding points.[6]

As for SBRs, Whitfield and Buur (2014) assert that three important conditions must be met if a state-business tie is to function well: (1) the mutual interests of ruling politicians and capitalists are served; (2) the rapport between ruling politicians and bureaucrats leads to efficient outcomes, specifically well thought-out policies; and (3) a desire for learning by bureaucrats and capitalists to enhance productivity. Nevertheless, in practice, insulation of bureaucrats from rent-seeking ruling elites is problematic, while politicians cannot be easily and institutionally sequestered from the particularistic pressures of the business sector. Moreover, ruling elites would certainly want to influence government policy-making processes to their own advantage as well as coerce bureaucrats into conforming with their ultimate political survival objective.

In discussions about different models of ties between states and businesses, three distinct forms have been identified: the 'invisible hand', 'helping hand' and 'grabbing hand'. The context of the invisible hand is one when the government plays an important role in providing public policies that cater to the needs of businesses, domestic and foreign, as well as the delivery of public goods and services, for example, high quality infrastructure and contract enforcement. The helping hand occurs when the state, recognising that the market needs support to function well, actively assists companies and promulgates policies that allow them to thrive. A grabbing-hand situation arises when the state is less well-organised or pursues its own agenda, leading to problems such as corruption.[7]

---

[6] For an in-depth discussion about these issues, see Maxfield and Schneider (1997), te Velde (2010) and Sen (2013).

[7] See Shleifer and Vishny (1993) for a review of these models. See also Frye and Shleifer (1997). For a discussion of these concepts from the perspective of China, see Kang, Hillman and Gu (2002). Studies have noted the concept of the 'iron hand', a case where the state attempts to kill off companies to serve the interests of firms linked to political elites (see, for example, Shleifer and Vishny 1993). There was no evidence of the iron hand in the case studies.

New State-Business Relations, New Trends

When assessing China's investments in Malaysia, a new trend was noted in the nature of SBRs: huge SOEs that function as MNCs were constructing business ties with GLCs to implement major projects conceived by these two governments. What was evident was that of a shift, from public-private partnerships to 'public-public partnerships', an outcome of the mandate by two governments to companies they own to jointly implement projects. In these public-public partnerships, where projects were implemented by SOEs and GLCs, there were no disputes with privately-owned companies as these governments decided how projects were to be shaped. Issues concerning funding of these projects appeared to have little bearing on public-public partnerships as they were supported primarily by China-based SOE-type financial institutions.

Evidently, a theoretical review is required of SBRs. In these new trends, clearly palpable also in other parts of Southeast Asia, since the key companies involved are SOEs or GLCs, with two governments authorising investments and executing projects through them, public-private partnerships were no longer a crucial dimension of state-business ties. In these new SBR forms, investment decision-making patterns differ because, in these public-public partnerships, governments are not dependent on private firms to take up policy incentives. Governments can shape investments in their own way, without worrying if private firms will respond to policy incentives to invest. In these public-public partnerships, the two governments can also determine how–or if–private sector involvement is to be handled in projects funded by them. The choice of private firms is, normally, decided by the two governments, depending on the project involved.

Although these SOE-GLC links that constitute foreign-domestic business joint ownership are common in state-state, state-state-private and state-private ties, power is not equitably distributed between these enterprises. Decision-making authority lies primarily with the large MNC-type SOE, suggesting also a shift in structural power, from private firms to the Chinese government. One reason for this shift is that China has extraordinary outreach and a potentially huge impact on developing economies by funding major projects, implemented by SOEs with technological know-how to deliver outcomes of high value. Crucially too for China, through these public-public partnerships, SOEs secure entry into numerous core sectors in developing economies.

However, strategic variations exist in terms of investment patterns by enterprises from China, as the case studies will point out. Moreover, as Fig. 1.3 indicates, private firms from China along with GLCs from Malaysia jointly run projects. A large number of companies from China, both SOEs and private firms, also function alone in Malaysia, and in a range of sectors. Big businesses, though not necessarily always as capital controllers, still exist among Chinese firms, seen particularly in the digital economy sector. In this sector, when private firms own enormous technical knowledge, they can exert much power over foreign governments by deciding if they should invest. This is particularly true when these private enterprises can act as advisors to the governments of host economies, as in the case of Jack Ma's Alibaba in Malaysia. This is also seen in the case of other technology-based companies such as Tencent and Huawei. Alibaba was heavily courted by the Malaysian government to help develop a Digital Free Trade Zone (DFTZ), an area dedicated to providing a whole range of services needed to ensure the speedy delivery of goods through e-commerce.[8] The DFTZ is closely linked to Malaysia's endeavour to keep abreast with the Industrial Revolution 4.0 (IR4.0), while there is now talk of a 'Digital Silk Road'.[9] One private-private tie that benefited Malaysia occurred when China's Geely teamed up with Malaysia's DRB-HICOM Bhd to revive the ailing Malaysian car project, Proton. It is unclear though if the Malaysian supply chain comprising domestic small- and medium-scale enterprises (SMEs) that had long participated in the Proton project will benefit from its revival with Geely's participation.[10]

One cautionary note is required here about private enterprises from China: the argument has been made that lack of state ownership does not imply no state control or state direction. In fact, large outward investments by leading Chinese private enterprises still need state approval, rather than mere registration (see de Graaff and van Apeldoorn 2018).

---

[8] See the case study on the DFTZ for an in-depth assessment of the conception and implementation of this project.

[9] For a discussion on the Digital Silk Road and its impact on Asian economies, see *The Diplomat* 30 April 2019. See also: https://thediplomat.com/2019/04/chinas-digital-silk-road-a-game-changer-for-asian-economies/.

[10] Interestingly too, foreign SMEs are keen to participate in this supply chain involving the production of Proton model vehicles which can further deprive domestic firms from participation in this automobile project. See the case study on Proton for details about the involvement of Geely, indicating here a private-private venture.

In other words, besides firm-specific interests, Chinese private companies must fulfil state-specific obligations before they are allowed to invest overseas. Due to close control and direction by the state, Chinese private firms can act as key functionaries of the state, similar to Chinese SOEs. Meanwhile, according to Tang (2017), Beijing also seeks to control top Chinese private developers to strike a balance between encouraging outward investments to support its BRI and preventing an unbridled exodus of capital that may destabilise its currency. Crucially too, state-business ties may involve business elites who are dominant corporate figures, but they remain subservient to the strong state.

In these different forms of state-business ties, as well as among firms functioning alone, one core feature is that of financial-industrial linkages, with financing provided by Chinese SOEs. A key issue emerged from this assessment of ventures in Malaysia by enterprises from China. The funding of these projects, including those that are BRI-based, was not by the multi-lateral-based AIIB, but by policy-based financial institutions such as the Export-Import Bank of China and China Development Bank, as well as state-owned commercial banks like the China Construction Bank. The role of China's policy-based banks in large state-state, state-state-private and state-private projects indicated an endeavour by this government to ensure that its foreign developmental-based projects proceeded unperturbed. However, while financing was available from China, the Malaysian government was aware that such fund flows could backfire, particularly if the loans taken are not repaid if these projects do not generate the expected revenue.

The institutional architecture that shaped policy planning in these projects is important as it provides insights into how the government–in some cases, both governments–shaped or re-shaped the way production networks and supply chains were created, an outcome expected of large-scale projects. In this institutional architecture, new public policies were conceived, and regulatory processes were eased, to facilitate implementation of projects, particularly those that were driven by state-state, state-private and state-state-private-based joint-ventures. What can be gleaned from these new forms of SBRs, facilitated through an enabling institutional architecture is the issue of complementarity. In this institutional architecture, business-based institutions, i.e. SOEs and GLCs, as well as those involving private enterprises and state-based enterprises, play different roles to facilitate implementation of these ventures. The case studies draw significant attention to the issue of institutional complementarity in ventures,[11] specifically where SOEs and GLCs are key actors.

These production networks and supply chains, led by Chinese SOEs and involving SMEs in Malaysia, can have a bearing on the volume of transfer of technology in key sectors. In different SBRs, the way technology transfers occur, leading to Malaysian SMEs learning by doing, can vary. In projects led by SOEs, with heavy government backing that allows for spending in costly research and development (R&D), high technological development projects, etc., this can lead to important structural transformation. Malaysian enterprises could well employ newly-acquired knowledge to develop their own expertise in key sectors, allowing them to move up the technological chain. Another dimension of this issue of learning by participating in joint-ventures with SOEs that offer high technological content is that Malaysian GLCs will emerge as major players in the industrial sector. However, these GLCs have a very limited presence in the technology sector.[12]

Importantly too, learning by participating in projects created by investments by Chinese SOEs may not always benefit domestic firms. In the electronics sector, for example, imports from China are increasingly coming through supply chains. This suggests that China is taking over larger chunks, or more value-added segments, of the electronics supply chain. This is one consequence of the different pace of technological advancement by China and supply chain countries like Malaysia.[13]

And yet, unlike private sector MNCs from the West that obsess over protecting their intellectual property rights, Chinese enterprises, whether state- or private-owned, have been open to the transfer of their home-grown technology to the enterprises of the host countries. In offering to make this transfer, Chinese enterprises are complying with their government's directive to export their technology to host countries. By this means, firms in the host countries will come to be locked into China's industrial eco-system. However, whether transfer of Chinese technology

---

[11] For a review of the concept of institutional complementarity, see Hall and Soskice (2001). See also the works of Whitley (1999) and Amable (2003).

[12] For an in-depth discussion of the poor participation of Malaysian GLCs in the technology sector, see Gomez et al. (2017).

[13] A more recent study shows China producing more of the intermediate goods used in the supply chains (Lund et al. 2019: 65).

can occur depends on the technological capability or depth of human capital of the host countries.

New State-Business Relations: Core Implications

The rise of SOE-GLC ties, emerging from a surge in fund flows from China into Southeast Asian countries after the introduction of the BRI, draws attention to the crucial point of changing forms of state intervention, clearly manifested in novel forms of SBRs. There are potentially positive outcomes from these state-state ties and re-configured SBRs, including:

a. construction of an institutional infrastructure that can facilitate trade;
b. promotion of key industries to speed up industrialisation;
c. nurturing of SMEs in Southeast Asia, an extremely important endeavour as they constitute the largest segment of the corporate sector in a country. In Malaysia, for example, SMEs comprise 98% of the corporate sector;
d. financing of research and development (R&D) as well as expensive and potentially risky technologically-based industries that the private sector would fear treading into; and
e. creation of regionally- and globally-based supply chains and production networks that can foster the rise of entrepreneurial domestic firms.

However, in these new SBRs, there are grave policy concerns as there are unclear boundaries between these governments and their SOES/GLCs, with little evidence of an arms-length relationship between them. Since two governments, collectively, can determine how the enterprises they control should function, a particularly problematic issue can emerge when such SBRs operate in a political system where the level of transparency and accountability is low. Indeed, based on findings from this study of SBRs, what is evident is the centrality of politics in decision-making in state-state, state-state-private and state-private ties which profoundly shape developmental outcomes.[14] Who governs in these SBRs can differ from project to project, depending on the type of state-business nexus that has been created. The economic goals, as well as the politics, of the states of China and Malaysia determine how these diverse forms of SBRs function.

In this study, an in-depth assessment is provided of FDIs by companies from China in the Malaysian economy. The primary focus of this study is to assess the implications of state-state ties that inform investment flows into Malaysia that also contribute to new forms of SBRs. The outcomes of these investments, implemented through different SBRs, on the evolution of the Malaysian economy are examined here. This volume provides case studies of companies, i.e. GLCs, SOEs and private firms, from Malaysia and China in manufacturing and services-based projects. The case studies offer a look into how China's SOEs and private enterprises function when they enter the Malaysian economy, with a review of the features of their corporate ventures with different types of Malaysian firms. The insights obtained provide important clues into the implications of burgeoning state-state ties through China's implementation of the BRI.

The selection of the case studies was based on projects that constituted what has been classified in this study as ties that are state-state, state-state-private, state-private, private-private, as well as projects involving a private enterprise or an SOE from China. The projects assessed are solely in the manufacturing and services sectors. These two sectors were selected for in-depth assessment as they provide insights into how state-state ties have contributed to the development of a range of projects involving a variety of firms, both Malaysian and Chinese. The selection of the case studies was based as well on the type of project involved, specifically to ensure that these enterprises were involved in different industries within the manufacturing sector. While most government- and journalistic-based reports have captured the pre-entry situation of the flow of investments by China into Malaysia, there has been little or no assessment of the post-entry outcomes or of the problems that have emerged during the implementation of projects by Chinese companies.

---

[14] Leftwich (2000) makes a particularly strong argument about the centrality of politics in developmental process, including those involving state-business ties.

Through these case studies, the institutional architecture through which SBRs function will be examined, with particular focus on determining where power lies in decision-making, with specific focus on the apex of the political system. An assessment will be undertaken to determine if there are deliberation councils, as well as coordination between them if they have been established. Evidence will be sought of the prevalence of mechanisms of transparency and accountability in the governance system, when decisions were taken to implement these projects. In the institutional architectures that exist, key issues will be reviewed: is there flow of accurate and reliable information between the government and business sector? Is there reciprocity and credibility within these institutional architectures? Indeed, is there mutual trust between the government and business in these newly-forged SBRs?

Other core issues will be assessed, specifically to determine if public-private partnerships are crucial for the development of new industries in the industrial sector. Through the case studies, the different forms of state intervention, including the rise of public-public-led-type investments, can be assessed. One key issue to be determined is whether the creation of an infrastructure to promote key industries and support the rise of SMEs has occurred through state-state ties.

CHAPTER 3

Chinese Investment Case Studies from Malaysia

SECTION 1: JOINT-VENTURES

A. Private-Private Venture

Case Study 1: Proton: Aiding the Ailing Malaysian Car

In 2017, the Malaysian automotive industry had 27 vehicle manufacturers producing passenger cars, commercial vehicles and two wheelers.[1] This industry contributed 4%, or RM40 billion, to Malaysia's Gross Domestic Product (GDP) that year. This industrial sector has 641 parts and components manufacturers and about 53,000 after-sales businesses, employing around 736,600 workers in the country. It is estimated that nearly 80% of the parts and components manufacturers within the economy are home-grown, Malaysian-owned companies.

Proton is Malaysia's national car, initiated by Mahathir Mohamad in the 1980s during his first administration as Prime Minister, from 1981 till 2003, as a method to create and develop industrial linkages between companies in different sub-sectors, as well as to nurture *Bumiputera*[2] entrepreneurs. Proton has received considerable government support

---

[1] Information obtained from the Malaysia Automotive Robotics and IoT Institute (MARii) (undated).

[2] Bumiputera, which means 'sons of the soil', is the term used in reference to ethnic Malays and other indigenous peoples. Of Malaysia's 32 million multi-ethnic population in 2019, Bumiputeras accounted for 65%, Chinese 26%, Indians 8% and the rest comprising other ethnic groups.

since its incorporation, even after Mahathir ended his first tenure as Prime Minister in 2003.

Proton was able to garner a large share of the domestic market in its early years due to tariff protection, a weak public transportation system and a growing middle class. In 1993, Proton's domestic market share was 74%.[3] However, Proton's market share started to fall with the introduction of a second national car, Perodua,[4] effectively a Daihatsu car, and the eventual removal of tariff protection under the ASEAN Free Trade Agreement (AFTA). Exports have been negligible throughout Proton's history as the company's focus has been on the domestic market. However, Proton failed to secure a major share in the domestic market, despite considerable government support in the form of grants, tax exemptions and non-fiscal assistance, amounting to RM13.9 billion since 1985.[5]

When it was incorporated, Proton was majority-owned by a newly-created GLC, Heavy Industries Corporation of Malaysia Bhd (HICOM), with Mitsubishi, its Japanese partner, holding a minority interest. Mahathir had used partnerships comprising GLCs and foreign multinationals to nurture heavy industries, including Proton. Mahathir encouraged such partnerships because he claimed that private domestic firms were reluctant to participate in industrial projects of this sort due to the large investments required and their lack of technological expertise (Jomo 1994). In 2005, Mitsubishi divested its shares to Khazanah Nasional Bhd, Malaysia's sole national sovereign wealth fund. As Proton's performance

---

[3] EU Delegation to Malaysia, 2012. Malaysia: The Malaysian Automotive Sector. https://rafiziramli.com/wp-content/uploads/2013/03/auto_sector_my_jan_12.pdf.

[4] In the Perusahaan Otomobil Kedua Bhd (Perodua) project, launched in 1993, the ownership pattern of this enterprise differed significantly from that of Proton. Although the government owned a stake in Perodua, the primary decision-makers in this enterprise were Japanese firms and a Chinese-controlled publicly-listed enterprise. Perodua was introduced to produce small-compact automobiles and its shareholders when it was established were the government-owned firms UMW and PNB Equity Resource Corporation, Japanese enterprises Daihatsu and Mitsui, and a publicly-listed Malaysian company, MBM Resources. MBM Resources, a Chinese family enterprise, is the lead domestic firm in this joint-venture. Toyota Japan owns a 51% stake in Daihatsu Japan and has an interest in UMW, giving the company a significant interest in the Perodua project. The Perodua project, unlike the Proton car venture, emerged as a major enterprise with growing capacity to export its products abroad (Gomez 2012: 69–71).

[5] *The Edge*, 1 November 2017. How much did Geely pay for the 49.9 percent Proton stake, asks MP. https://www.theedgemarkets.com/article/how-much-did-geely-pay-499-proton-stake-asks-mp.

continued to deteriorate, in 2012, it was acquired by DRB-HICOM, a Malaysian conglomerate, with diversified interests, in the automotive, services and property development sectors, owned by a well-connected tycoon, Syed Mokhtar Al-Bukhary.[6] In the automotive sector, DRB-HICOM is involved in the manufacture, assembly and import of motor vehicles, including contract manufacturing and distribution for Japanese and European brand cars.

DRB-HICOM's acquisition of Proton did not stop the latter's slide in its domestic market share of the car sector. Instead, Proton's continued dismal performance impinged negatively on the profitability of the DRB-HICOM group.[7] Since the losses incurred by Proton were a serious drain on DRB-HICOM's resources, it voiced its intention to sell its stake in this car project, but no buyer could be found.[8] The government subsequently had to extend a soft loan of RM1.5 billion to bail-out Proton as funds were needed to pay the vendors.[9] In return for the loan, Proton had to produce a transformation plan, one that included identifying a well-known strategic partner that would help it penetrate the international market, besides recapturing its domestic market share.

In May 2017, China's Zhejiang Geely Holding Group Co. Ltd acquired from DRB-HICOM a 49.9% stake in Proton. According to DRB-HICOM, its 49.9% interest in Proton was valued at RM700 million. However, Geely paid DRB-HICOM RM170.3 million in cash and gave Proton the rights to its best-selling model, the Boyue SUV (sports utility vehicle), which was valued at RM600 million.[10] Although DRB-HICOM retained a 51% stake in Proton, it divested its interest in Lotus Advance Technologies to Etika Automotive Sdn Bhd, an enterprise owned by

---

[6] For a review of Syed Mokhtar's vast business interests in Malaysia, see http://www.kinibiz.com/story/issues/58876/the-sprawling-empire-of-syed-mokhtar-albukhary.html.

[7] *Kinibiz*, 30 May 2014. Proton a drag on DRB-HICOM earnings. http://www.kinibiz.com/story/corporate/88542/proton-a-drag-on-drb-hicom%E2%80%99s-earnings.html.

[8] DRB-HICOM looking to sell entire Proton stake. https://paultan.org/2016/08/08/drb-hicom-looking-to-sell-entire-proton-stake-report/.

[9] *The Star Online*, 9 April 2016. Proton gets soft loan from Govt. https://www.thestar.com.my/business/business-news/2016/04/09/proton-gets-soft-loan-from-govt.

[10] There was evidently some controversy over the price paid by Geely for its interest in Proton. For a report on this acquisition, see *The Edge*, 1 November 2017. How much did Geely pay for the 49.9 percent Proton stake, asks MP. https://www.theedgemarkets.com/article/how-much-did-geely-pay-499-proton-stake-asks-mp.

Syed Mokhtar (49%) and Geely (51%).[11] Proton had acquired Lotus, the British sports car marque, in 1996.[12]

Proton's sale went through an international bidding process which included site visits, in order to ascertain the appropriate foreign strategic partner,[13] based on the criteria stipulated by the government. Geely was chosen because it agreed to two key conditions. First, the Proton name would be retained. Second, Geely would endeavour to ensure Proton reclaimed its position as the top-selling automobile in Malaysia, thereby enabling it to regain its lost domestic market share. Geely's history of turning around Volvo[14] served as evidence that it had the ability to achieve the objective of reviving Proton.

Geely also proposed to expand Proton's car sales beyond Malaysia, matching the government's and DRB-HICOM's ambitions. Geely announced that it planned to sell 500,000 units by 2027, implying more employment opportunities for Proton. Geely further undertook to provide Malaysia access to 'green technology' for automotive manufacturing as the government aspired to produce electric vehicles. Geely was then already producing electric-based vehicles. Importantly too for Malaysia, the planned Proton Research and Development (R&D) Centre was to be recognised as one of the Geely Group's Centres of Excellence. This Chinese enterprise assured the Malaysian government that training opportunities would be provided to Proton engineers, to allow them to learn the technologies being developed at its four design studios and five R&D plants. Proton was to be the right-hand drive (RHD) manufacturing hub for Geely. Proton's plant in Tanjung Malim, in the state of Perak, would get to assemble Volvo cars.[15]

After the Geely group's acquisition of this enterprise, a new set of directors were appointed on 29 September 2017 to the boards of PROTON Holdings, Proton Edar Sdn Bhd, the local distribution arm,

---

[11] *The Star*, 23 June 2017. Zhejiang Geely buys Proton, Lotus stakes for RM1bil. https://www.thestar.com.my/business/business-news/2017/06/23/drb-hicom-and-zhejiang-geely-ink-final-contract-for-proton-lotus/.

[12] Ibid.

[13] *New Straits Times Online*, 28 May 2017. DRB-HICOM chief: Sale of Proton stake to Geely isn't 'selling out'. https://www.nst.com.my/news/exclusive/2017/05/243320/drb-hicom-chief-sale-proton-stake-geely-isnt-selling-out.

[14] See Chen, Wang and Young (2015) for details on Geely's acquisition of Volvo.

[15] Ibid.

and Perusahaan Otomobil Nasional Sdn Bhd (PONSB). Three nominees from Geely Holding joined each of these boards. They were Daniel Donghui Li, the Executive Vice President (VP) and Chief Financial officer (CFO) of Geely Holding; Dr. Nathan Yuning, the Executive VP of International Business of Geely Holding; and Feng Qing Feng, the Group VP and Chief Technical officer (CTO) at Hong Kong-listed Geely Auto. DRB-HICOM was represented by Syed Faisal Albar, who chairs these three boards, as well as Amalanathan Thomas and Shaharul Farez Hassan, who were previously part of the company's senior management team. Dr. Li Chunrong, who had strong credentials and considerable experience in the automotive sector, joined PONSB as Chief Executive Officer (CEO). This indicated a devolution of power, as well as control over Proton, by the Malaysians to a partnership comprising Geely, the technology provider.

Geely is China's first privately-owned auto manufacturer. In 2017, Geely was reported to be ranked at number five among the top ten best-selling Chinese automakers in China. This list of firms in the automotive sector included SOEs. Geely started producing cars in 1997 and entered the export market in 2003.[16] Geely Auto was listed on the Hong Kong Stock Exchange in 2005. This listing provided Geely Auto access to the capital market in Hong Kong to finance its expansion plans, making it less dependent on bank loans from China.

Geely's ambitions included transcending China's competitive domestic market by producing safe, eco-friendly and energy-efficient cars for the world. In line with these ambitions, Geely announced its 'Go Global' strategy in November 2007. It then began a series of strategic acquisitions, beginning in 2009, with the purchase of the Australian transmission maker DSI (Drivetrain Systems International) for A$47.4 million.[17] DSI was then the world's second largest manufacturer of automatic transmissions. Three years later, in 2010, Geely acquired Volvo from Ford for US$1.5 billion. In 2013, Geely bought Manganese Bronze, renaming it the London Taxi Company. A year later, the Geely group purchased Emerald Automotive, an enterprise specialising in light-weight, low emission and long-range hybrid commercial vehicles.

---

[16] See http://global.geely.com/history/.

[17] Geely group's remarkable rise via tech takeovers. https://www.carsifu.my/news/geely-groups-remarkable-rise-via-tech-takeovers.

Geely's mode of strategic asset acquisitions to bolster its competitive reach is not peculiar to this enterprise. Other Chinese companies had been similarly—and increasingly—undertaking mergers and acquisitions (M&As). In 2005, Chinese companies accounted for a mere 7% of Asia Pacific's M&A activities.[18] This more than tripled to 23% in 2010, and then increased even further to 50% in 2015.

Importantly too, Geely was able to use its acquisitions to add value to its production network which helped enhance its profits. For example, Volvo was a loss-making company when Geely acquired it from Ford. Geely has since been able to revive Volvo's sales in Europe, the United States and China, with the latter becoming its biggest market.[19]

Geely also invested in R&D to enhance its domestic and global competitive position. This was cogently demonstrated by its investments in design studios and R&D plants. Geely's R&D has reportedly yielded 14,000 patents and the group is apparently recognised as one of China's top ten brands for intellectual property and independent innovation.

Geely's purchase of Proton was attributed to two key factors. The Proton partnership was a means for Geely to access a very large Southeast Asian market, one currently dominated by Japanese car manufacturers. Three million new vehicles are reportedly sold annually in the region.[20] This was not how the Proton-Mitsubishi partnership functioned. In this Malaysian-Japanese partnership, Mitsubishi was competing with Proton for market share in the region. Understandably, this reduced the incentive by Mitsubishi to transfer technology in key components to develop new Proton models (Tong and Lim 2012). For Geely, Southeast Asia is seen as a market for right-hand, instead of left-hand, vehicles, as in China. Geely plans to use Proton to shift towards the production of right-hand vehicles, a turn that requires significant re-engineering works. Second,

---

[18] J.P. Morgan, undated. China's increasing outbound M&A: Key drivers behind the trend. https://www.jpmorgan.com/global/insights/chinas-key-drivers.

[19] Volvo & Geely: The unlikely marriage of Swedish tech and Chinese manufacturing might that earned record profits. https://www.forbes.com/sites/pamelaambler/2018/01/23/volvo-geely-the-unlikely-marriage-of-swedish-tech-and-chinese-manufacturing-might-that-earned-record-profits/#12126bdf4ecc.

[20] *Nikkei Asian Review*, 9 October 2017. Proton's new CEO sets course to revive Malaysian carmaker. https://asia.nikkei.com/Business/Proton-s-new-CEO-sets-course-to-revive-Malaysian-carmaker.

Geely had the opportunity to buy Lotus, which will facilitate its entry into the sports-car segment to complement its current production line.

For Malaysia, the sale of Proton to Geely marked yet another attempt to transform the then long-flagging national car company into a global player. In 2017, Proton had pressing needs, namely to shift from loss-making to profitability, to improve its domestic market share, to penetrate the export market and to achieve technology transfer that would enable it to join the list of global automotive players, or, at least, acquire a strong reputation for itself in Southeast Asia.

This need to be profitable meant that for the sake of the development of Proton, the Malaysian state had to relinquish its enormous influence over this enterprise to its technology partner, Geely. There was an urgent need to jump-start the shift towards profitability via the introduction of new models, at lower costs, as well as improve customer service. Proton's transformation started quickly with the introduction of the first 'new' Proton model in late 2018, an SUV named the Proton X-70, based on Geely's Boyue, and designed by Volvo designer Peter Horbury.

Total registrations for the X-70 from its launch in late 2018 till the first quarter of 2019 stood at 9906 units, a massive increase in sales by Proton. Subsequently, by the end of the first quarter of 2019, over 25,000 bookings were received.[21] By end 2019, Proton had moved to bring in completely-knocked-down (CKD) units of the Proton X-70. Proton would then replace the production of the X-70 model with the assembly of these CKDs, in order to lower the price of the car and increase its local content. Proton also launched four upgraded versions, in terms of modifications of the body of the model and/or changes in some parts of existing models, in order to recapture its market share.

Cost-cutting and technology-upgrading processes were initiated with a revamp of the dealers and vendors. Selected Proton dealers were brought to China to learn from the Geely and Volvo showrooms. Meanwhile, collaborations between vendors and vendor partners from China were fostered to bring in FDI and new technology for parts producers. These new collaborations will supply automotive parts to Proton and, eventually, to the world by participating in production networks. Selected

---

[21] Proton ends Q1 2019 with record figures—2,979 X-70 sold in March, highest ever SUV sales in M'sian history. https://paultan.org/2019/04/02/proton-ends-q1-2019-with-record-figures-2979-x70-sold-in-march-highest-ever-suv-sales-in-msian-history/.

Malaysian vendors will be able to meet international standards and cultivate export capacity by participating in these global production networks, thus gaining economies-of-scale. Local content in new Proton models is scheduled to increase progressively over time. Batches of selected engineers were also being sent to Geely's automotive center in Ningbo for training and to upgrade their technical knowledge.

Proton had invested RM1.2 million by mid-2019 to upgrade its plant in Tanjung Malim for the production of the CKD version of its 'new' SUV model.[22] This plant has a production capacity of 150,000 units per annum, and it targeted to commence operation by September 2019. DRB-HICOM obtained RM944 million cash through the sale of its waste management outfit which provided it with funds to underwrite existing or future investments.[23] However, future developments for Proton, be it in terms of research or infrastructure development, was to be financed out of the RM1.88 billion loan obtained from China Construction Bank (CCB) in April 2019.[24] CCB is one of the four largest state-owned banks in China. This loan is to finance Proton's plans to become the number one automotive brand in Malaysia and the number three in Southeast Asia by 2027.

Proton commenced its internationalisation journey when it signed a licensing and technical assistance agreement with Pakistan's Alhaj Automobile in 2019, to build a manufacturing plant in Karachi with an initial investment of US$30 million. This plant will assemble and distribute Proton cars for the Pakistani market.

It appears that the sale of Proton to Geely is mutually advantageous. Part of the reason lies in the commercial terms of the transactions, where a deal was achieved to profit both companies. After all, Proton had to generate profits to contribute to the profitability of Geely. Turning around Proton therefore constituted a crucial component of this transaction, thereby giving the foreign CEO the space to execute a transformation

---

[22] DRB-HICOM, 2019. Annual report 2019. https://www.malaysiastock.biz/GetReport.aspx?file=AR/2019/7/31/1619%20-%201135231272488.pdf&name=DRBHICOM_AR2019_PART%202A.pdf.

[23] *The Edge*, 13 August 2018. Asset sale to fund Proton's operation. https://www.theedgemarkets.com/article/asset-sale-fund-protons-operations.

[24] Proton secures RM1.88 billion loan from China Construction Bank for R&D and Infrastructure Development. https://www.theedgemarkets.com/article/proton-secures-rm188b-loan-china-construction-bank-rd-and-infrastructure-development.

programme. The other reason, and possibly the more important one, was the inability of politicians to interfere to upset the deal. Political interference in Proton was a characteristic feature of much of this company's chequered history. This suggested much autonomy on the part of Geely in the management of Proton. The financial transaction occurred in 2017, before Mahathir, the brainchild of the national car project, returned to power in May 2018. After returning to power, following the general election in 2018, Mahathir was forced to accept the sale of Proton to Geely, due also to his support of China's investments in Malaysia.

B. State-State Venture

Case Study 2: Malaysia-China Kuantan Industrial Park (MCKIP)
The Malaysia-China Kuantan Industrial Park (MCKIP) is a state-state facilitated project, which was launched in February 2013, prior to the announcement of the BRI. The MCKIP is the first industrial park in Malaysia to be accorded national status.[25] As Khor (2013) noted, 2013 was an important election year in Malaysia and the park is located in Pahang, the home state of the then Prime Minister, Najib Razak. Kuantan is geographically located within what the government has classified as the East Coast Economic Region (ECER), an area that covers 51% of the less developed parts of the east coast of Peninsular Malaysia.[26] The MCKIP was established to foster greater inflows of investments from China to Malaysia as a means to rebalance investment relations between the two countries. Malaysia was then a net exporter of capital to China.

---

[25] MCKIP receives RM10.5 billion of new investments, 8,500 job opportunities for the rakyat in the ECER. ECER media room announcements, 5 February 2013. https://www.ecerdc.com.my/en/media_releases/mckip-receives-rm10-5-billion-of-new-investments-8500-job-opportunities-for-the-rakyat-in-ecer/.

[26] Abdullah Ahmad Badawi, during his term as Prime Minister from 2003 to 2009, had launched what he referred to as economic corridors. These five corridors were Iskandar Malaysia (located in the state of Johor), Northern Corridor Economic Region (NCER) (encompassing Perak, Penang, Kedah and Perlis), ECER (covering primarily the underdeveloped states of Pahang, Kelantan and Terengganu), Sabah Development Corridor (SDC) and Sarawak Corridor of Renewable Energy (SCORE). For an insight into the development of these corridors by the government, see https://www.mida.gov.my/home/malaysia-economic-corridors/posts.

These investments, in turn, were meant to facilitate economic development in the ECER, thereby enabling the region to catch up with the more developed west coast of Peninsular Malaysia.

After the launch, Malaysia and China signed the First Five-Year Programme for Economic and Trade Cooperation (2013–2017), in October 2013.[27] The programme aimed to strengthen economic relations between the two countries. Under this programme, the China-Malaysia Qinzhou Industrial Park was to be established as the sister industrial park in China to the MCKIP. This new cooperation initiative was underpinned by strong trade relations between the two countries. China had been Malaysia's biggest trading partner for four consecutive years, while Malaysia was China's largest trading partner among ASEAN countries for five years in a row prior to 2013.

The key player in this investment project is the Master Developer of MCKIP, which is a joint-venture between a consortium of Malaysian enterprises (51%) and a China-based grouping (49%). China's consortium consists of two provincial SOEs, China Guangxi Beibu Gulf International Port Group (CGBGIP) (95%) and Qinzhou Jinqu Investment Company Ltd (QJIC) (5%). CGBGIP was established in Nanning in 2007, dealing primarily with the construction and operation of ports, railway and roads. In 2013, it operated four ports in southern China, i.e. the Fangchenggang, Qinzhou, Tieshan and Beihai ports. These four ports reportedly handled about 200 million freight weight tonnes (fwt) of cargo in 2012 (Tham 2019). QJIC, established in 2012, is wholly-owned by the Qinzhou City Development and Investment Group Co Ltd which belongs to the Qinzhou City Government (Khor 2013). It is involved in the operation and management of state-owned construction assets.

The Malaysian consortium was initially supposed to be led by a state-state-private partnership. It first comprised SP Setia Bhd, one of the largest GLCs in the property development sector,[28] Rimbunan Hijau Group, a well-connected private sector conglomerate of Sarawak origin, and the Pahang state government. However, in early 2014, both SP Setia and Rimbunan Hijau withdrew from the project (Ngeow 2019). In April,

---

[27] The Ministry of Foreign Affairs of the People's Republic of China, 2013. China and Malaysia. https://www.fmprc.gov.cn/mfa_eng/wjb_663304/zzjg_663340/yzs_663350/gjlb_663354/2732_663468/.

[28] SP Setia had emerged as a leading privately-listed property developer. In 2011, it was taken over by Permodalan Nasional Bhd, a major state-controlled investment fund.

SP Setia sold its stake in the consortium, worth RM9.7 million to IJM Land Bhd, which is part of the conglomerate, IJM Corporation Bhd, another GLC and one of Malaysia's largest construction companies.[29] IJM planned to use MCKIP as a means to further diversify its business, into industrial property development, as well as, geographically, enter a new territory, Kuantan, on the east coast of the peninsula.

In the Malaysian consortium, IJM Land holds a 40% equity, while Kuantan Pahang Holdings Sdn Bhd and Sime Darby Property Bhd together hold 30% and the Pahang state government holds the remaining 30%. According to *Nikkei Asian Review*,[30] GLCs and government entities, such as Permodalan Nasional, Employees Provident Fund, Kumpulan Wang Persaraan and Urusharta Jamaah Sdn Bhd, have invested in IJM, accounting for 44.2% of the company's shares as at 2019. IJM, however, remains independently run as a private publicly-listed company, with no representation of the government on its board. Hence, the Malaysian consortium is represented by a mix of companies, privately-owned, federal government-owned (Sime Darby Property) and state of Pahang-owned. There was an important reason for the involvement of a GLC owned by the Pahang state government in the Malaysian consortium. The issue of the use of land is a matter decided by state governments in the Malaysian federation. The involvement of the Pahang state government and Sime Darby Property was to ensure access to the land needed for the Park. The land for developing MCKIP in 2014 measured approximately 729 acres.[31]

When this project was launched, the investment commitments in MCKIP were announced. Guangxi Beibu Gulf International Port Group was to invest RM5 billion for three projects in the Park. Another RM3 billion was to come from the Guangxi Beibu Gulf International Port Group and IJM for the Kuantan Port expansion project. RM2.5 billion was to be provided by the Master Developer of MCKIP.[32] Based on these

---

[29] MCKIP in http://www.kuantanport.com.my/en_GB/industrial-area/mckip/.

[30] *Nikkei Asian Review*, 2019. IJM Corp. Bhd. https://asia.nikkei.com/Companies/IJM-Corp.-Bhd.

[31] IJM, 2014. Annual report 2014. https://cdn1.i3investor.com/my/files/st88k/5215_IJMLAND/annual/2014-03-31/5215_IJMLAND_AnnualReport_2014-03-31_IJMLAND-AnnualReport2014_2116961018.pdf.

[32] MCKIP receives RM10.5 billion of new investments, 8,500 job opportunities for the rakyat in the ECER. East Coast Economic Region (ECER) media room announcements,

investment commitments, the motivation for SP Setia and Rimbunan Hijau to sell their stakes in the project to IJM became clear. With Guangxi Beibu Gulf International Port Group and IJM investing in both the Port and Park, this would facilitate synergies between the projects. Moreover, the expansion of the Kuantan Port required an expansion of the hinterland via MCKIP, in order to provide for the needed industrial activities to stimulate demand for cargo (that is, imports and exports) through the port (Tham 2019). The Park and Port projects were thus viewed as inter-related and complementary, rather than as independent operations.

The Malaysian federal government supported the development of the MCKIP and Kuantan Port for two reasons. First, the Park has national status. Second, the federal government holds a special rights share in the privatised Kuantan Port as it is a federal port. Consequently, the government provided RM1.7 billion worth of incentives and infrastructure support. The financial package included the development of the primary infrastructure in MCKIP, such as the construction and upgrading of a direct road linking MCKIP to the Kuantan Port, as well as the necessary water, electrical and telecommunications facilities to support the development of the Park.[33] Federal government support included an allocation of RM1 billion to build a new 4.7 kilometre breakwater, considered one of the longest in the world, for the creation of a sheltered harbour that is necessary for the expansion of Kuantan Port as it is not a natural port. As for the special incentive that was offered, this entailed a 100% tax exemption of up to 15 years for selected approved investors, which is five years more than the normal tax-free incentive.

At the launch of the MCKIP, a strategic document was signed, the Framework Agreement on Financing Cooperation, between the Master Developer of MCKIP and China Development Bank Corporation,[34] one of the top ten banks in China. This bank has reportedly funded 38 BRI

---

5 February 2013. https://www.ecerdc.com.my/en/media_releases/mckip-receives-rm10-5-billion-of-new-investments-8500-job-opportunities-for-the-rakyat-in-ecer/.

[33] Malaysia-China Kuantan Industrial Park (MCKIP) seals investments worth RM1.58 million from China and Malaysia. ECER Media room announcement, 31 May 2016. https://www.ecerdc.com.my/en/media_releases/malaysia-china-kuantan-industrial-park-mckip-seals-investment-worth-rm1-58-billion-from-china-and-malaysia/.

[34] Ibid.

projects in 2018.³⁵ It appeared that at least a portion of the RM2.5 billion needed to develop the Park, based on the Framework Agreement on Financing Cooperation, was to be provided by a loan from China Development Bank Corporation. As for IJM, as a publicly-listed firm, it had a policy of borrowing strictly in ringgit terms for its projects within Malaysia, using local banks. However, IJM switched to borrowing from China Construction Bank (Malaysia) Bhd. as it was offered a lower interest rate.³⁶ China Construction Bank was granted a banking licence in 2017 to facilitate financial cooperation and exchanges between Malaysia and China.

The resulting form of partnership indicated that while the MCKIP remained a state-to-state directed project, the Malaysian state, while continuing its support for the project had relinquished decision-making to IJM, the operational partner. However, China retained its control over the project through its SOE. While financing from China was supported by SOE banks, the Malaysian partner, as a publicly-listed GLC, used commercial loans. This suggested that while the project can be used to support the interest of the Chinese state, the Malaysian side had to be answerable to IJM's shareholders, in terms of the financial returns to the project as a business venture, rather than as a developmental project of the state.

Over time, the land allocated for the development of MCKIP has expanded progressively, with the expansion of IJM's land bank and an increase in demand from investors. By 2017, the land bank consisted of three parcels: MCKIP 1 (which consists of 1200 acres of land), MCKIP 2 (1000 acres) and MCKIP 3 (800 acres).³⁷ MCKIP 1 is designated for high technology and heavy industries, while MCKIP 2 was designated for high-end and high technology industry development. MCKIP 3 was

---

[35] HSBC Global Asset Management, undated. Belt, Road and Beyond: Understanding the BRI opportunity. https://www.fiduciaryinvestors.com/wp-content/uploads/sites/61/2019/03/Belt-road-and-beyond-understanding-the-BRI-opportunity.pdf.

[36] Private communication, 1 October 2019.

[37] Hong Kong Trade Development Council (HKTDC), 16 May 2017. Prospects for the Malaysia-China Kuantan Industrial Park and Kuantan Port.. http://economists-pick-research.hktdc.com/business-news/article/Research-Articles/Prospects-for-the-Malaysia-China-Kuantan-Industrial-Park-and-Kuantan-Port/rp/en/1/1X000000/1X0AA0CO.htm.

designated for multi-purpose development projects, including light industries, commercial property, residential areas and tourism parks. By June 2019, the land bank had expanded to 3500 acres.[38]

However, IJM's equity interests in the three parcels are not the same. This is because the Master Developer for MCKIP is engaged only in the development of the first parcel of land. Therefore, IJM has only 20% effective interest in MCKIP 1, while the Chinese counterpart has 49% equity interest.[39] In the case of the other two parcels, MCKIP 2 and MCKIP 3, IJM is a 60% shareholder, while the Chinese counterpart has the remaining 40% equity interest. IJM is also involved in the execution of the MCKIP project, in terms of developing the infrastructure of the park. As a listed company, IJM can fund its operations by issuing bonds in the capital market, securing term loans, revolving credits and other borrowing facilities.

The preponderance of Chinese investors in the Park is due to its promotion in China by the East Coast Economic Region Development Council (ECERDC).[40] However, approval for investment incentives continued to be under the jurisdiction of the Malaysian Investment Development Authority (MIDA), a federal-based institution under the Ministry of International Trade & Industry (MITI). At the operational level, in terms of actual investments that flowed into the Park, IJM depended heavily on Guangxi Beibu, its Chinese partner, to promote the project in China. In fact, Guangxi Beibu was tasked to introduce investors for a steel mill plant, an aluminium processing plant and an edible oil processing plant in MCKIP, when the port's expansion plans were announced in

---

[38] Ministry of International Trade and Industry (MITI), 2019. Media release: The 4th Joint Cooperation Council (JCC) Meeting on Malaysia-China Kuantan Industrial Park (MCKIP) and China-Malaysia Qinzhou Industrial Park (CMQIP). https://www.miti.gov.my/miti/resources/Media%20Release/Media_Release_The_4th_Joint_Cooperation_Council_(JCC)_Meeting_on_Malaysia-China_Kuantan_Industrial_Park_(MCKIP)_and_China-Malaysia_Qinzhou_Industrial_Park_(CMQIP).pdf.

[39] IJM, 2018. 34th AGM Minutes, 28 August 2018. https://www.ijm.com/sites/default/files/extract-minutes/ir_minutes_agm_180828.pdf.

[40] See Media Room, September 2016, Promoting investment opportunities in ECER, Malaysia: ECERDC eyeing bigger slice of Chinese Investments from CAEXPO 2016. https://www.ecerdc.com.my/en/media_releases/promoting-investment-opportunities-in-ecer-malaysiaecerdc-eyeing-bigger-slice-of-chinese-investments-from-caexpo-2016/.

2013.[41] IJM is principally a construction enterprise with little or no experience in investment promotion, especially in manufacturing. In fact, besides China, there are, as yet, no investors from other countries in the Park. Nevertheless, these inflows can also be attributed to push factors since China's manufacturers have been gradually shifting their production offshore, in response to domestic pressures such as increasing costs, excess capacity as well as increasingly stringent environmental controls. It is therefore not surprising that the first investment project is in steel, where there is considerable excess capacity. IJM's role is to facilitate investment approval, as well as to assist investors secure access to Malaysia's tax incentives. IJM therefore plays an intermediary role between the investors and investment approval and granting of incentives in Malaysia. This intermediary function is driven by profits, rather than any developmental objective, since IJM is a publicly-listed enterprise that is accountable to its shareholders for its investments in the MCKIP and the expansion of the port.

By the end of 2019, about 80% of the land in MCKIP 1 had been taken up by investors. As for MCKIP 2, the second parcel in the Park development, 30% of the land was earmarked for one investor. This investor, the largest to date at the Park, is Alliance Steel (M) Sdn Bhd. The production site of just this steel-based enterprise from China covers 710 acres, or nearly 60% of MCKIP 1. The second investment project is a concrete spun pile manufacturing plant that has also commenced operation. As at June 2019, MCKIP had 10 committed projects, with a total investment of about RM18 billion, which will contribute to creating 20,000 jobs.

The main products manufactured in the Park are steel, porcelain ware and ceramic tiles, spun concrete piles for manufacturing and battery manufacturing for energy efficient vehicles. When a trade war erupted between the United States and China in 2018, this conflict apparently stirred interest among China's manufacturers to relocate their production to Southeast Asia, including to Malaysia.[42] It appears that China's investments will continue to dominate at the MCKIP.

---

[41] Alliance Research, 2013. News flash: IJM Corporation (construction). https://klse.i3investor.com/files/my/ptres/res13543.pdf.

[42] *Focus*, 1 October 2018. Trade war adds FDI lure to Kuantan. http://www.kuantanport.com.my/en_GB/trade-war-adds-fdi-lure-to-kuantan/. Accessed 29 November 2018.

The products produced at the Park will inevitably have an export component since China is used to producing on a very large scale, while Malaysia's domestic market is relatively small.[43] Imports of raw materials, capital equipment and intermediate goods, such as machinery and parts, will also feed freight demand at the expanded capacity at Kuantan Port. Phase 1 of the deep-water terminal at the expanded Port commenced operation in the fourth quarter of 2018.[44] The port's annual handling capacity will be doubled to 52 million tons, when the new deep-water terminal (Phase 2) is completed. Kuantan Port subsequently obtained Free Zone port status. On 1 April 2019, the port established the Free Trade Zone.

The immediate gain from the investment projects at the MCKIP is employment. The investors were also required to provide training for Malaysian workers employed to operate the equipment and machinery used at the new plants, as in the case of Alliance Steel. These workers are expected to acquire new skill sets, in terms of operating highly sophisticated machineries.

Through these foreign investments, Malaysia aims to gain from technology transfer. The main forms of technology transfer lie in training and development, as well as through domestic sourcing of component products from Malaysian companies. However, by the end of 2019, there was no evidence of technology transfer through domestic sourcing of intermediate goods. It remains to be seen if these Chinese firms are willing to increase domestic sourcing and help local SMEs learn new technologies to develop their capacity to meet the specifications of the new manufacturing facilities at MCKIP. Ultimately, it depends on costs considerations, which are biased towards Chinese suppliers as they have economies-of-scale, which local producers do not have unless they export.

Alternatively, the Chinese partner at the Park may act as an intermediary in getting Chinese suppliers to relocate their production to Malaysia. This can lead to another round of investments from China's SMEs that

---

[43] Interview at IJM, 29 October 2018.

[44] Ministry of International Trade and Industry (MITI), 2019. Media release: The 4th Joint Cooperation Council (JCC) Meeting on Malaysia-China Kuantan Industrial Park (MCKIP) and China-Malaysia Qinzhou Industrial Park (CMQIP). https://www.miti.gov.my/miti/resources/Media%20Release/Media_Release_The_4th_Joint_Cooperation_Council_(JCC)_Meeting_on_Malaysia-China_Kuantan_Industrial_Park_(MCKIP)_and_China-Malaysia_Qinzhou_Industrial_Park_(CMQIP).pdf.

are producing the requisite intermediate inputs. This will depend on the changes in China's production conditions and costs, as they evolve over time.

C. *State-Private Venture*

Case Study 3: Digital Free Trade Zone (DFTZ)
E-commerce as a growth strategy was launched by the Najib Razak administration, before the fall of his government during the 14th General Election in May 2018. The unexpected election result did not lead to a change in focus by the new government, about the need to develop e-commerce in the country. E-commerce is part of Malaysia's National Policy in IR4.0, 'Industry Forward' (Industry4WRD), that was launched by Prime Minister Mahathir Mohamad on 31 October 2018, although the plan was initially formulated by the Najib administration. The IR4.0 policy aims to help transform Malaysia's manufacturing sector by embracing the technological revolution that is changing production and consumption patterns throughout the world. In the case of consumption, e-commerce is a key disrupter, suggesting that producers need to reconfigure the way they interact with consumers, be it as business-to-business (B2B) or business-to-consumer (B2C) transactions.

The Najib administration had engaged Jack Ma of Alibaba as an advisor in November 2016 to develop e-commerce in Malaysia, leading to the idea of creating a Digital Free Trade Zone (DFTZ). The DFTZ is essentially a zone dedicated to a whole range of services needed to ensure the speedy delivery of goods via e-commerce. The DFTZ is scheduled to be made available over a staggered timeline. The zone is the first of Jack Ma's internet-based trading platform or electronic-World Trade Platform (e-WTP). Specifically, an e-Fulfilment[45] hub, a satellite services hub and an e-Services Platform are being developed over two phases, with the first phase undertaken by Pos Aviation, a government enterprise, at a cost of RM60 million. These funds were used to upgrade and renovate the former Low-Cost Carrier Terminal (LCCT) for the development of e-fulfilment facilities of the DFTZ. The DFTZ is already operational.

---

[45] This encompasses warehousing and order fulfilment, shipping logistics and last mile delivery in an e-commerce value chain.

This pilot project serves mainly as the e-fulfilment hub of Lazada,[46] an online shopping outlet acquired by Alibaba in 2016. There are, however, on-going efforts by Pos Aviation to attract other platform players to the DTFZ.[47]

In the second phase, Cainiao Network, the logistics arm of Alibaba, is affiliating with Malaysia Airports Holdings Bhd (MAHB), in a greenfield investment to establish an ASEAN e-commerce hub near the Kuala Lumpur International Airport (KLIA). This investment will be located within the KLIA Aeropolis, an aviation hub that MAHB is planning to develop around KLIA. It is centred around three core clusters, namely air cargo and logistics, aerospace and aviation, as well as a locale for meetings, incentives, conferences and exhibitions (MICE) and leisure.

Cainiao has selected five cities in the world to become its global hubs: Hangzhou, Dubai, Kuala Lumpur, Liege and Moscow.[48] These global hubs are being developed to lower logistics costs and shorten delivery time for meeting Alibaba's stated goal of single day-delivery within China and 72-hour delivery across the globe. They will also serve to provide the necessary logistics infrastructure needed to drive the traffic for Alibaba's e-commerce platforms such as Taobao, Tmall, AliExpress, as well as other services, including its e-payments tools such as Alipay—essentially the whole evolving Alibaba ecosystem in e-commerce. The ASEAN e-commerce hub is an important component in Alibaba's foray to establish and strengthen Jack Ma's group's e-commerce footprint in Southeast Asia, as part of the digital silk route that he is aiming to initiate, along the BRI countries.[49]

A new joint-venture company named Cainiao KLIA Aeropolis Sdn Bhd was established in 2017 from this partnership. This joint-venture, 70% (or RM144.7 million) owned by Cainiao and 30% (or RM62 million) by

---

[46] Lazada is an international e-commerce enterprise owned by Alibaba. In April 2016, Alibaba acquired 51% of Lazada from Rocket Internet and further increased its shareholdings to 83% in 2018.

[47] Interview with Pos Malaysia at DFTZ, 10 May 2019.

[48] Cainiao reveals plans for five global logistics hubs. https://www.aircargonews.net/cargo-airport/cainiao-reveals-plans-for-five-global-logistics-hubs/.

[49] *The Malaysian Reserve*, 1 August 2019. KLIA Aeropolis DFTZ Park on schedule, to be launched next June. https://themalaysianreserve.com/2019/08/01/klia-aeropolis-dftz-park-on-schedule-to-be-launched-next-june/.

MAHB, has a paid-up capital of RM206.7 million.[50] Media announcements indicate that the JV will invest approximately RM800 million to develop the e-commerce hub.[51] This is apparently the amount allocated by MAHB for its capital development expenditure such as infrastructure facilities, equipment and systems for the park.[52]

According to MAHB'a annual report for 2017, Cainiao HK is a wholly-owned subsidiary of Cainiao Smart Logistics Network (BVI) Ltd, which is in turn wholly-owned by Cainiao Smart Logistics Network Ltd (Cainiao Cayman). Cainiao Cayman is an affiliate of Alibaba Group Holding Ltd., which is publicly-listed on the New York Stock Exchange. The Alibaba group is reported to be cash rich, with nearly US$30 billion in cash and cash equivalent in its balance sheet.[53] This implies that there should not be any problem for the parent company to fund the development of the hub and it is not as dependent on SOE financing, as in the case of other projects reviewed in this study.

MAHB has a monopoly over the operation, management and maintenance of the 39 airports in Malaysia, six of which are international. MAHB is also a GLC, as Khazanah Nasional and other state investment agencies such as Permodalan Nasional and the Employees Provident Fund, are its majority shareholders with an estimated 44% equity interest.[54] MAHB also owns stakes in Turkey's Sabiha Gokcen International (ISGA), and two airports in India, Delhi International and New Hyderabad International. However, MAHB is reportedly divesting part of its investments in the Turkey and Hyderabad airports, reportedly to

---

[50] *MAHB News*, 3 November 2017. http://mahb.listedcompany.com/news.html/id/633197.

[51] *The Malaysian Reserve*, 10 April 2018. MAHB-Cainiao JV to invest RM800m for DFTZ expansion. https://themalaysianreserve.com/2018/04/10/mahb-cainiao-jv-to-invest-rm800m-for-dftz-expansion/.

[52] See https://www.thestar.com.my/business/business-news/2018/04/09/mahb-allocates-rm800mil-klia-aeropolis-dftz.

[53] *The Edge*, 19 August 2019. What's behind Alibaba's quest to raise USD30 billion?

[54] KLIA Aeropolis concept master plan, released on 23 May 2016. http://www.kliaaeropolis.com/sites/default/files/MAHB%20Air%20Cargo%20&%20Logistics%20Brochure-7%20(130519).pdf.

raise the funding it needs to invest in the development of the KLIA Aeropolis.[55]

The current fiscal constraints encountered by the Malaysian government suggests that its funding for the current and future development of the KLIA Aeropolis is unlikely to occur. The government's budget in 2019 indicates that the Mahathir administration plans to use private funding to co-finance all airport developments, or upgrading, as it is planning to establish an airport real estate investment trust (airport REIT).[56] Thirty percent of the REIT is to be sold to private institutions to obtain funds for airport development in the country.

MAHB had apparently been planning to develop the 10,000 acres of vacant land surrounding the KLIA, the largest international airport in Malaysia, since 2008. However, this did not occur as MAHB's concessions for the airports under its care were due to expire in 2034. Give that the concession phase was to expire within what was considered a short period, the commercial development of the land surrounding the airport was not seen as a viable venture.[57] However, in April 2019, MAHB was granted an extension of these concessions until 2069 by the new administration, indicating Mahathir's support for the continuation of the KLIA Aeropolis project.

The ASEAN e-commerce hub is expected to be completed by June 2020 and it is targeted to be operational by September 2020.[58] It occupies 40% of the 150 acres of land within the Aeronautical Support Zone 1 (ASZ1) of the KLIA Aeropolis. When completed, it will house a cargo terminal, sorting centres, warehouses and fulfilment centres, which are essential logistics operations for facilitating regional e-commerce activities.

As in all hub/park development projects, land is an important component. This is because the land is usually leased to investors for the development of their respective projects. The Malaysian partner in any

---

[55] https://www.nst.com.my/business/2018/02/332153/hlib-maintains-buy-call-mahb-target-price-rm10.

[56] https://www.edgeprop.my/content/1441069/budget-2019-mahb-airport-reit-formation-way-govt-securitise-its-infra-assets.

[57] *The Edge*, 9 June 2019. The beginning of the end for Subang's Terminal 2. https://www.theedgemarkets.com/article/beginning-end-subangs-terminal-2.

[58] *The Edge*, 31 July 2019. KLIA Aeropolis DFTZ to be completed by June next year. https://www.theedgemarkets.com/article/klia-aeropolis-dftz-be-completed-june-next-year.

joint-venture hub/park operation is the primary agent for acquiring the land needed for park development. For this purpose, MAHB entered into a sub-lease annexure of 60 acres of land in Bandar Lapangan Terbang Antarabangsa Sepang, with a lease of 30 years, commencing 2 May 2018 and expiring on 2 May 2048. Under the terms of the sub-lease annexure, it is automatically renewed until 10 February 2069, effectively giving the 60-acre land a 51-year lease.[59] Apart from land, the local partner's role is to liaise with Malaysian authorities for approvals, any needed permits as well as to secure government incentives.

According to MAHB, its strategic partnership with the Alibaba Group is estimated to double air cargo volume from around 650,000 tonnes to 1.3 million tonnes annually, as well as double freighter flights by 2028.[60] This joint-venture is expected to generate RM11.8 billion in GDP cumulatively (2020–2029) and support over 129,700 job-years during this period. The division of labour is estimated to be 37% of skilled workers (operations manager, facilities technicians, logistics planner, etc.) and 52% semi-skilled (equipment operators, assemblers, service and sales workers, etc.). Given Alibaba's critical role as a strategic partner, the facilities at the e-commerce-hub will, in all likelihood, be mainly utilised by this Chinese multinational and its related businesses and partners. These facilities will also compete directly with the logistics facilities under Pos Aviation that were developed in the first phase of the DFTZ.

Understandably, MAHB's vested interests are air cargo volume and the increased utilisation of its KLIA airports as these will serve to increase the profits of the company. Alibaba claims that the e-commerce initiatives will help Malaysian SMEs to export, an important objective of the DFTZ. While it is true that e-commerce can facilitate exports by lowering the fixed costs incurred in exporting, it does not ensure that SMEs can export as this ultimately depends on the competitiveness of these domestic enterprises. Malaysian SMEs will have to contend with Chinese SMEs and other exporters on all of Alibaba's e-commerce platforms, as well as other e-commerce platforms. More importantly, the trade facilitation facilities on the Malaysian side improves the time needed for processing imports and exports, thereby making it easier and faster for imports to enter

---

[59] *MAHB News*, 3 November 2017. http://mahb.listedcompany.com/news.html/id/633197.

[60] Private communication with MAHB, 27 August 2019.

the country (Tham and Kam 2019). By contrast, all Malaysian SMEs exporting to China and the rest of the world have to undergo the customs procedures of all importing countries, which is not harmonised. SMEs will still have to learn the customs clearance procedures and processes of each importing country before they can successfully enter each of these countries.

While this project is aligned with the e-commerce goals of the country, as well as the government's desire to develop the KLIA as a regional transportation hub,[61] both MAHB and Cainiao are answerable to their respective shareholders. Although the commercial interests of both companies, which in this case represents the private sector in China and a GLC in Malaysia, can be met through co-investments in this project, the national interests of Malaysia, such as enabling domestic SMEs to export through the DFTZ initiative, is not necessarily guaranteed.[62] The underlying objective of the Malaysian state is to spur e-commerce development, but this goal is articulated narrowly as in getting SMEs to export. Alibaba's interests are first, to use Malaysia as part of its global trading and logistics hub, especially for the region and second, to get SMEs listed on its platforms. However, whether these SMEs get to export or not will depend on the initiatives of these enterprises. This is because the shift from offline to online selling requires a different skills-set, one that these Malaysian SMEs have to develop. Such skills can be obtained by undergoing training on the digitalisation of their business, including digital marketing and selling. This type of training comes at a price, to be charged by Alibaba, or other providers. Importantly too, and ultimately, Malaysian SMEs must develop competitive products which can be sold to the world if they hope to benefit from their participation in the DFTZ project.

---

[61] See the report by the Malaysian Industry Government Group for High Technology (MIGHT 2015).

[62] MATRADE, the export promotion agency of Malaysia, is directly involved in the promotion of SMEs in e-commerce for the purpose of export, with the use of financial incentives for qualified companies.

Section 2: Chinese Firms
A. Private Chinese Venture

Case Study 4: Jinko: Private Investment in Solar Manufacturing
Malaysia's Third Industrial Master Plan (IMP3: 2006–2020) had identified Solar Photovoltaics (PV) as one main renewable technology for the country. PV is expected to be the lead industry among all renewable energies. The photovoltaic industry was, in fact, listed as one key sector to support in the Economic Transformation Programme (ETP) that was launched in 2010. Under the ETP, Malaysia was targeted to be at the forefront in the manufacturing of PV technology by 2020, instead of being a mere assembler. The Economic Planning Unit (EPU), together with the World Bank, mapped out in 2011 the PV value chain to support this shift. This 2011 study recommended using this sector to attract foreign investments as well as develop a more coherent and integrated approach to nurture the upstream and downstream segments of PV technology, a mechanism to move up the value chain. In order to achieve this objective, Malaysia worked towards developing an entire PV or solar industry ecosystem; from research and development (R&D) and design to the production of metal silicon, polysilicon/ingots and solar wafer/cells, solar modules as well as system integrators, all with the use of foreign investments.

The Malaysian Investment Development Authority (MIDA), as the designated agency for investment promotion and approval, was tasked to attract foreign investments for the development of this ecosystem, using fiscal incentives, comprising tax holidays, investment tax allowances, reinvestment allowances, import duty exemptions and non-fiscal incentives such as a feed-in tariff scheme and a green technology funding mechanism. Malaysia's relatively low electricity and labour costs added to the locational advantages of the country for these types of investments. In 2008, Malaysia received RM12 billion that was targeted at the PV industries. Four prominent solar companies, First Solar, Q-Cells, Sunpower and Tokuyama, mainly from the United States, Taiwan, Germany and Japan, invested in Malaysia (EPU and World Bank 2011). By 2009, due to these foreign investments, Malaysia had become the third largest producer of PV, after China and Germany, overtaking Japan in just a year.

The US administration had implemented anti-dumping duties on the import of Chinese solar panels in 2012 (UNCTAD 2014). However, using a loophole in the final ruling, Chinese manufacturers circumvented these duties by importing cells manufactured in other countries and then assembled the modules in China. Consequently, Chinese manufacturers moved production abroad to places such as Malaysia, South Korea and Taiwan, to circumvent the retaliatory measures and at the same time, to lower costs by seeking out the lowest-cost markets. Penang in Malaysia emerged as one of the beneficiaries from this relocation, besides other countries in Southeast Asia such as Thailand.

JinkoSolar Technology Sdn Bhd is a subsidiary company of JinkoSolar Holding Co. Ltd. The parent company was founded by Xiande Li, Kangping Chen and Xianhua Li on 3 August 2007 and it is headquartered in Shangrao, China. It was listed in 2010 on the New York Stock Exchange. The parent company designs, develops, produces and markets photovoltaic products and provides solar system integration services. It focuses on vertically integrated solar power products manufacturing, from silicon ingots, wafers and cells to solar modules. Jinko has four production facilities in the world: Jiangxi and Zhejiang provinces in China, Portugal, South Africa and Malaysia.[63] The firm's manufacturing facility in Penang was established in 2015 to produce highly-efficient cells and multi-crystalline modules. According to Jinko, the manufacturing locations were chosen based on efficiency-seeking arguments as they are "in close proximity to our key resources and suppliers and provide us with easy access to skilled labor at competitive costs".[64]

A US$25 million combined trade-line agreement was signed between Jinko's Malaysian subsidiary and Malayan Banking (Maybank),[65] Malaysia's leading publicly-listed commercial bank and a GLC. In 2017, the International Finance Corporation (IFC)[66] announced its intent to channel US$60 million as funding for a US$100 million plan to upgrade the Malaysian subsidiary's existing solar cell production lines to produce

---

[63] https://www.prnewswire.com/news-releases/jinkosolar-production-facility-in-malaysia-begins-operations-300088449.html.

[64] "Preliminary Prospectus Supplement" (To Prospectus dated August 22, 2017). https://www.secinfo.com/d12TC3.yPE5.htm#lm2.

[65] http://ir.jinkosolar.com/node/7606/pdf.

[66] The IFC is a financial institution that offers advisory, investment and asset-management services to encourage the development of private enterprises in emerging economies. The IFC was incorporated in 1956 as the private-sector arm of the World Bank Group to advance economic development by investing in for-profit and commercial projects that contribute to the reduction of poverty as well as promote equitable development.

passivated emitter rear cells (PERC), a shift that was expected to boost energy conversion and cut down on system costs.[67] Jinko commenced mass production of PERC-based solar cells and modules in January 2017. It is reportedly in the process of upgrading its production lines at its manufacturing facilities in China and Malaysia.

The entry of Jinko in Penang was strongly supported by this state government and the federal-based MIDA.[68] Penang was chosen because it is Malaysia's hub for the semiconductor industry, which provides key inputs for the making of solar cells. In addition to the advantage of lower cost of labour that is available in the country, Penang has the added benefit of the availability of skilled engineers. The Penang state government and MIDA collaborated to secure solar-based investments. Moreover, obtaining foreign investments and creating employment opportunities are listed as key performance indicator (KPI) targets that both the Penang state and MIDA have to achieve. In particular, a Mandarin-speaking Chief Minister, Lim Guan Eng, facilitated the process. This, in turn, enabled the Jinko production facility to be completed and certified for production within two months.[69] This is crucial because China is accustomed to speedy implementation of projects.

MIDA provided tax incentives such as a 100% income tax break for 10 years, along with a 100% investment tax allowance for capital expenditures since this is a targeted sector for foreign investments. This has attracted not just Jinko to Penang, but other solar companies from China. For example, the Nasdaq-listed Chinese solar cell manufacturing company, JA Solar Holdings, also launched its first solar cell manufacturing facility in Penang in October 2015.[70]

Jinko's entry into Malaysia is a typical FDI story, whereby the state, through its designated institution, MIDA, facilitated the entry of foreign investors. In this case, the head of Penang state, cooperated with MIDA to ensure Jinko's smooth entry into Malaysia. Although MIDA's targeted investments, including the solar projects, are based on the development

---

[67] https://www.pv-tech.org/news/ifc-to-invest-us60-million-in-jinko-malaysia.

[68] https://www.eco-business.com/news/jinkosolar-build-cell-and-module-facility-malaysia/.

[69] https://www.prnewswire.com/news-releases/jinkosolar-production-facility-in-malaysia-begins-operations-300088449.html.

[70] https://www.pocketnews.com.my/2015/10/25/official-opening-of-ja-solar-in-bayan-lepas-penang-with-yab-lim-guan-eng/.

needs of the country, its performance requirements are based on a narrow set of goals which can be measured with ease, which are investment value and employment targets and, sometimes, export requirements. Local sourcing is difficult to measure and requires tracking over time. It is also difficult to ascertain if local sourcing has enhanced SME development in the industry. The omission of this key variable implied that local sourcing of key components, which is a critical component for technology transfer, is left to market forces, rather than directed by the state.

According to MIDA,[71] in 2015, 48 solar projects were implemented with a total investment of RM28.0 billion, to produce solar wafers, cells, modules and system components. Of this total, 95.3% were foreign, while another 4.7% was from domestic sources. These projects had created about 26,700 job opportunities. MIDA further reported that export and local sourcing activities undertaken by the top solar companies in Malaysia in 2016 were valued at RM11.1 billion and RM1.42 billion respectively. Apart from MIDA, the extent of local sourcing used in Malaysia was not reported anywhere else, so that the magnitude of local content used in Jinko's production and exports was unclear. One media outlet reported that the local content in First Solar was around 20–25% and confined to local services such as packaging, semiconductor management processes, ethylene-vinyl acetate polymer sheets and labelling.[72] Technology transfer through domestic sourcing of local components, especially key components of the production process, is an important channel as it would require local firms to meet international standards as well as the specifications of multinationals that are buying the product. Without local sourcing of components, technology transfer will be limited to training and skilling programmes and diffusion via labour turnover or when the trained workers leave the MNC to work for other firms or to start their own enterprises.

In MIDA's Investment Performance Report 2016, Jinko's additional investment of RM484.8 million to its initial investment of RM310 million in 2015, was described as quality investment because the expansion plan

---

[71] https://www.mida.gov.my/home/3532/news/malaysia-well-positioned-to-attract-more-solar-investments/.

[72] See, for example, *The Star Online*, 17 November 2011. First Solar intends to increase local content. https://www.thestar.com.my/business/business-news/2011/11/17/first-solar-plans-to-increase-local-content.

signified the investor's confidence in the local economy.[73] The number of additional jobs created with the expansion plans was reported to be 2552, compared to the initial employment of 1333 in 2015. The concern of the state was evidently on investment and employment, rather than local sourcing to ensure technology transfer.

Jinko has invested heavily in R&D to stay competitive. In 2017, it was ranked eighth in a sample of twenty key publicly-listed PV module manufacturers, spending a reported sum of US$45.2 million that year, an amount that was significantly more than the approximately US$23 million it spent in 2016.[74] Research and development laboratories located in Jiangxi and Zhejiang provinces and in Penang focus on enhancing the quality of solar products, improving production efficiency and increasing the conversion efficiency of the solar cells and modules. R&D is targeted at improving product quality to enhance competitiveness. This in line with the general trend of technology improvements in the country, which focuses more on improvements in quality rather than new products (Tham et al. 2016).[75] Jinko has reportedly moved to collaborate with Nanyang Technology University (NTU) in Singapore on the production of perovskite solar cells after a one-off funding for research at a Malaysian university.[76] By contrast, Jinko's award-winning new products are developed outside Malaysia. For example, Jinko's collaboration with Dupont in Europe enabled it to win the Intersolar Award 2019 in the Photovoltaics category. This award was for Jinko's Swan bifacial module with transparent backsheet, developed with DuPont.[77]

Meanwhile, in the United States, President Donald Trump's solar tariffs, which are universal tariffs, have negatively affected domestic exports of solar from Malaysia (Tham et al. 2019). Trump's measures have raised the possibility of investment relocation of solar production

---

[73] https://www.mida.gov.my/home/administrator/system_files/modules/photo/uploads/20170302155931_Slides%20Presentation%20Malaysia%20Investment%20Performance%202016.pdf.

[74] https://www.pv-tech.org/editors-blog/solar-manufacturing-industry-rd-spending-in-2017-hits-new-high.

[75] "Preliminary Prospectus Supplement" (dated 22 August 2017). https://www.secinfo.com/d12TC3.yPE5.htm#lm2 or ir.jinkosolar.com/static-files.

[76] https://www.pv-tech.org/news/jinkosolar-starts-perovskite-cell-rd-collaboration.

[77] https://www.prnewswire.com/news-releases/jinkosolar-wins-intersolar-award-2019-for-its-swan-bifacial-module-300852256.html.

from Malaysia to the United States to avoid these tariffs. Nevertheless, current operating cost conditions in Malaysia as well as its cumulative investments have continued to sustain Jinko's operations in Penang. There were no reports of relocations as of late 2019. Instead, Jinko expanded its R&D facilities in Penang in December 2019, to look beyond process technology.[78] This is in line with its increasing focus on R&D to improve efficiency, rather than just cost reduction,[79] presumably to diversify its risks with the on-going trade war.

Nevertheless, in June 2018, in response to the Trump tariffs, Jinko had apparently commenced plans to produce solar panels at a new factory in Jacksonville, Florida, using the solar cells from Malaysia.[80] Jinko also had plans to apply for an exemption to the cell import tariffs, to import the large-format solar cells that it makes in Malaysia for use in building solar modules at its Florida factory. Jinko hoped that the exemption would be granted since JinkoSolar is the only manufacturer in the world that makes these panels. The solar tariffs appear not to have hindered the manufacturing operations of Jinko in Malaysia.

A. *Private Chinese Venture*

Case Study 5: D&Y Textile (Malaysia) Sdn Bhd
D&Y Textile (Malaysia) Sdn Bhd's investment in Malaysia of US$200 million, located in the Sendai Industrial Park, in the state of Johor, represents a form of foreign direct investment that is entirely Chinese-owned and financed from China.[81] It is unusual among foreign investors that a parent company locates its high-tech manufacturing facilities outside its home base, with its ownership of high technology in Malaysia.

Malaysia's textile industry is quite matured, with low barriers to entry and a highly competitive environment. A major exporter of textiles and made-up garments since Malaysia adopted export-oriented industrialisation as a strategy in the 1970s, these goods combined was the

---

[78] http://taiyangnews.info/business/jinkosolar-builds-rd-center-for-tiger-panels-abroad/.

[79] https://www.pv-tech.org/editors-blog/jinkosolar_no_longer_the_rd_spending_laggard.

[80] https://www.thestar.com.my/business/business-news/2018/06/20/jinko-to-produce-solar-panels-in-florida-from-cells-imported-from-malaysia.

[81] Interview with a staff of D&Y on November 2019.

country's thirteenth largest export earner in 2018. The United States was the leading export market for Malaysia's textile products.[82] The major import source in 2016 was China.[83] Competition from emerging economies with lower production costs, such as China, has spurred Malaysian manufacturers to push up the value chain, by developing and improving processes, focusing on higher value-added products and improving efficiency through automation.

In 2018, 18 projects were approved in the textiles and textile products industry, with investments totalling RM851 million. Domestic investors took the lead, with RM566.3 million. Approved investments of RM398 million were concentrated in the production of primary textiles.

To accelerate the shift of the manufacturing and services sectors from labour-intensive to high value-added, knowledge-intensive and innovation-based industries, the Malaysian government introduced a new tax incentive, the Automation Capital Allowance (ACA) in 2015. Labour-intensive industries such as textiles are under this scheme. External developments also encouraged the relocation of firms in Malaysia and other Southeast Asian countries. Wages in China had risen significantly, due to demand factors and minimum wage hikes, putting pressure on domestic firms producing there.[84] In 2013, with the launch of the BRI, a new phase of 'going out' by Chinese enterprises began. More recently, with the beginning of the China-US trade war, Southeast Asian suppliers saw a chance to quickly replace China as a source of textiles import. China is the world's biggest textile supplier with its huge textile-manufacturing infrastructure. Malaysia, Indonesia and Bangladesh are expected to become key

---

[82] Malaysian Investment Development Authority, 2019. Malaysia Investment Performance Report 2018. https://www.mida.gov.my/home/administrator/system_files/modules/photo/uploads/20190315105335_MIDA%20IPR%202018.pdf.

[83] Ministry of International Trade and Industry, 2017. Textiles, apparel and footwear industry profile. https://www.miti.gov.my/miti/resources/4._Textile_Apparel_and_Footwear_Industry_.pdf.

[84] See, for instance, Yan, 2017. 'Made in China' is not so cheap anymore, and that could spell headache for Beijing. *CNBC*, 27 February. https://www.cnbc.com/2017/02/27/chinese-wages-rise-made-in-china-isnt-so-cheap-anymore.html. See also https://globalpayrollassociation.com/blogs/regional-focus/are-chinese-labour-costs-growing-too-high-after-latest-minimum-wage-hikes.

players in the global textile supply chain.[85] Firms located in these countries, including Chinese firms, can help push Malaysia into the centre of the world textile stage. These developments, together with heightened international and local competition, require Chinese enterprises to upgrade their production processes, adopt automation and look to investing in appropriate host countries.

This series of events set the stage for Chinese textile companies to invest in Malaysia, where offshore textile and garments production has a long history. The incorporation of D&Y, the Malaysian operation of the Daiyin Group, is an example of investment in the textile sector. This investment by the Daiyin Group was mainly driven by its desire to enhance efficiency.

Daiyin Group is a huge diversified enterprise with a particular interest in spinning, weaving, clothing manufacture and import and export trade. Established as the Tai'an Second Cotton Textile Factory in 1987, it was a state-owned enterprise, then restructured in 1994 as the Tai'an Daiyin Textile Co. Ltd., a joint-stock company with the state as a majority equity shareholder. In May 2003, when the ownership reforms were implemented, Tai'an Daiyin Textile Co. was transformed into a private company, after the sale of all state-owned shares in December 2003. The Daiyin Group, born as a state enterprise, had emerged as a private enterprise.[86] However, even without state ownership, as a former state enterprise, the Daiyin Group is well-connected with other SOEs of China; in other words, with the government.

The Daiyin Group's strong relationship with the Chinese state is most evident when assessing the machinery it uses in its Malaysia textile projects. The complete set of cotton spinning equipment for the second phase of the Malaysia project was obtained from China Hi-Tech, a textile equipment manufacturer and a 'yang qi' (central enterprise).[87] Given its

---

[85] *Daily Express*, 2019. Malaysia has potential to increase textile exports to US. Retrieved from http://www.dailyexpress.com.my/news/130478/malaysia-has-potential-to-increase-textile-exports-to-us/.

[86] info.texnet.com.cn, 2014. Fabric company: Is your R&D mechanism ready? http://info.texnet.com.cn/detail-499680.html.

[87] 'Yang qi' refers to a wholly state-owned or state-holding enterprise that is directly managed by the central government (the state council) or entrusted to a state-owned assets supervision and administration institution to perform the functions of investor. Its leading group is directly managed by the central government or entrusted to the organisation department of the central committee, the State-owned Assets Supervision and

comprehensive strength in textile machinery, China Hi-Tech ranks first in China, indeed also a world leader. It is a multinational enterprise group with considerable strengths in the fields of textile trade, new fibre materials, commercial automobiles and construction machinery, financial investment and cultural industry.

China Hi-Tech has cooperated with the D&Y Group for more than 20 years. Under the BRI, these two enterprises have combined forces to develop their respective enterprises. The textile investment in Malaysia is committed to building China Hi-Tech's demonstration base, as well as a service and spare parts centre in Malaysia for its complete set of cotton spinning equipment.[88]

The origins of D&Y's investment can be traced to the visit to Malaysia by the Chairman of the Daiyin Group, Zhao Huanchen, in October 2013. Zhao was part of a Chinese business delegation led by President Xi to attend the Malaysia-China Economic Summit. At this summit, the development of Daiyin Group's Malaysian textile project was strongly promoted.[89]

What motivated D&Y's investment in Malaysia? Steven Cheng, the General Manager of D&Y, was quoted as saying: 'Malaysia had a good historical relationship with China. Raw materials here are cheaper than in China and the infrastructure here is robust. With the domestic textile situation in China increasingly competitive, Malaysian production cost is becoming lower than in China. Also, it is very convenient to send our goods to export from Malaysia.'[90] This points to Malaysia having a locational advantage for D&Y's products. An additional factor was possibly the low cost of energy.[91] In addition, Malaysia did not impose tariffs on

---

Administration Commission (SASAC) of the state council, and other central ministries and commissions. For a list of 'yang qi', see http://www.sasac.gov.cn/n2588035/n2641579/n2641645/index.html.

[88] info.texnet.com.cn, 2018. D&Y Textile Malaysia Phase II project officially put into production. http://info.texnet.com.cn/detail-700504.html.

[89] Daiyin Group, 2019. History. http://www.daiyin.com/Article.asp?ArticleID=7.

[90] YouTube, 2016. China invests in Southern Malaysia. https://www.youtube.com/watch?v=hfcM-g65SkA.

[91] Daiyin Group, 2018. Gao Yong, Secretary of Party Committee of China National Textile and Apparel Council, went to D&Y Textile (Malaysia) Sdn Bhd for research and guidance. http://www.daiyin.com/newsdetail.aspx?NewsId=75&cateid=23.

the import of raw cotton, a critical input, unlike some countries. This helped keep the price of raw cotton imports manageable for D&Y.

A second set of factors is related to the Chinese government's strategy of seeking out markets. However, D&Y's Malaysian investment was conceived in 2013, preceding the launch of the BRI. Nevertheless, in the context of China's BRI, the country's latest version of its 'going out' strategy, as pronounced in the 2015 'Guideline of the State Council on Promoting International Cooperation in Production Capacity and Equipment Manufacturing',[92] entails exporting an entire industry ecosystem to different countries to help them build a more complete industrial system and enhance manufacturing capacity.[93] China's textile industry is a good fit for this strategy. Being an integrated sector, its textile industry has a complete industrial system, with various categories and considerable technical levels, and accounts for a considerable amount of global processing and export. Moreover, in recent years, China's so-called 'new normal' has pushed its textile enterprises into transforming and upgrading their core competitiveness.

A third reason for D&Y's entry into Malaysia is that this private enterprise, given its roots in the state sector, continues to comply with government priorities such as the 'going out' strategy. However, even former state enterprises, once 'privatised', enjoy a great deal of autonomy in their day-to-day operations, much like private enterprises in the rest of the world. This is an illustration of the unclear separation between state enterprises and private firms in China, making the form of state-business relations that are created even more complex.

D&Y's fourth reason for this venture was that Malaysia's Promotion of Investment Act offers tax incentives in the form of 'pioneer status', or investment taxes allowances, to firms manufacturing several textile products.[94] D&Y's products fall within the category 'yarn of natural or man-made fibres'. With respect to the choice of Kulai to locate its factory,

---

[92] The State Council of the People's Republic of China, 2015. Guideline of the State Council on promoting international cooperation in production capacity and equipment manufacturing. http://www.gov.cn/zhengce/content/2015-05/16/content_9771.htm.

[93] Belt and Road Portal, 2016. International capacity cooperation. https://www.yidaiyilu.gov.cn/info/iList.jsp?tm_id=126&cat_id=10030&info_id=2175.

[94] Malaysian Investment Development Authority, 2019. Textiles and textile products. https://www.mida.gov.my/home/textiles-and-textile-products/posts/?lg=ARB.

D&Y's management favoured the state of Johor due to its close proximity to Singapore and its excellent port facilities. Other major factors that contributed to the decision to locate its plant in Kulai included the relatively low price of land and transportation costs.

A crucial reason for D&Y's investment was Malaysia's membership in the Trans-Pacific Partnership (TPP), a regional grouping which did not include China. By producing from a TPP member country, D&Y's products could secure preferential access to the market in the United States in particular. This was due to the yarn-forward requirement in the TPP, whereby the yarn used to produce the clothing for export to member countries, had to be sourced from within member countries.[95]

On the Malaysian side, the entry of an export-oriented high-tech player in a long familiar sector carried the prospect of greater international competitiveness in an area of major exports that had been governed by an established institutional infrastructure. The long history of the textile sector in Malaysia had led to a set of incentives for industry players, with clearly defined roles for firms and government agencies. The regional environment likewise offered positive prospects from the formation of the ASEAN Economic Community, of which Malaysia is a member.

Given these positives, D&Y's total investment of US$400 million was a sizeable greenfield investment, undertaken in three phases to build a special yarn project with a total scale of 500,000 spindles. D&Y's core objective is to build a world-class modern textile industrial park. The construction of the first phase of a 100,000 gauze ingot plant commenced in March 2014. It was completed and began production in May 2015. The construction of the second phase of a 120,000 gauze ingot plant project began in early 2017. After more than a year of plant construction, installation and commissioning, the project was put into production in May 2018. This project saw the introduction and use of the world's most advanced textile equipment to produce high-grade yarn with world-class quality.

This form of foreign investment has several implications for Malaysia. First, the entire project consists of greenfield investments from China. This implies not merely an absence of Malaysian financial commitments to the project, but also the absence of debt obligations. Second, from China's perspective and by Cheng's own admission, his company appears

---

[95] Malaysian Investment Development Authority, 2019. Investment performance Report 2013. https://www.mida.gov.my/env3/uploads/PerformanceReport/2013/IPR2013.

not to have benefited from Malaysia's preferential trade policies with the region and the world. This is because its market is only focused on China and Malaysia. Moreover, Malaysia's market is quite small. However, the company hopes to use Malaysia as a springboard to expand its market into Southeast Asia. Thus, China may not only take advantage of Malaysia's regional trading connections, but also use this country as an export platform to third countries, as well as avoid the anti-dumping duties imposed by the United States. This is in addition to D&Y being able to sell Malaysia its textile equipment and eventually to draw the country into its industrial eco-system for textiles. In this sense, D&Y is able to take advantage of ASEAN's regional institutional infrastructure to enhance its export competitiveness.

For Malaysia, an immediate impact of D&Y's investment was that it would generate employment in Johor.[96] Crucially too, this investment earned for Malaysia an estimated US$350 million in foreign exchange by exporting all products from the Johor plant.[97] Since the investment funds came entirely from China, they represent incremental financial resources for Malaysia that can boost its industrial competitiveness through the installation of advanced technologies processes in Malaysia. However, Malaysia does not have the capacity to benefit from technology transfer, constrained as it is by D&Y's high degree of automation. This is a technology that Malaysia lacks. Even if it offered to train locals, D&Y can only teach them how to operate the machines. Another issue is that it is likely that the short-term impact of D&Y's presence on the local textile industry is to heighten competition and to incentivise the purchase of Chinese equipment. To some extent, the latter is occurring, by establishing a demonstration base and service and spare parts centre. Still, Malaysian suppliers could acquire industrial upgrading through the purchase of advanced equipment from China. To the extent that many of these suppliers are SMEs, upgrading of this sector will eventually occur. This is also a type of transfer of technology that is expected to appear eventually. Importantly too, to the extent that Malaysia has become a part of China's textile value chains, it will be able to capture a significant portion of the value-added that is generated.

[96] The condition for granting a manufacturing license is that a third of all employees should be locals.

[97] Johor State Investment Centre, 2017. Johor—The pride of Malaysia. https://jsic.gov.my/download-attachment/1229.

What factors would bring China and Malaysia together to clinch a deal of this kind, given that China may benefit disproportionately? D&Y's reliance on state-owned China Hi-Tech for its technology suggests that China's 'going out' strategy is much more than just about gaining international competitiveness for Chinese enterprises by selling Chinese products. China's strategy, as revealed by the 'Guideline of the State Council on Promoting International Cooperation in Production Capacity and Equipment Manufacturing', is also about deepening the national development initiative by promoting the adoption of China's machinery and production processes in countries that are recipients of its investments. Chinese investments serve to integrate the host countries' industries, industrial systems and manufacturing capabilities into the China's industrial eco-system.[98] This is very much a part of the BRI, one that represents a new phase of the two decades old 'going out' strategy.[99]

Consequently, the China National Textile and Apparel Council (CNTAC) encouraged leading textile enterprises to accelerate their pace of going out, as well as to invest in textile raw material bases and processing bases and research and development centres. These enterprises were also encouraged to expand their marketing channels abroad, so as to maintain their competitiveness and promote industrial restructuring in host countries through the allocation of transnational resources. The second phase of the project would also effectively drive the export of Chinese textile machinery equipment. This, in turn, played a positive role in promoting the going out of China's textile machinery industry. Likewise, China Hi-Tech's demonstration base and service and spare parts centre can play a role in promoting industrial restructuring in Malaysia.

While this approach has many positives for China and its SOEs, Malaysia sees itself as being the host of a high-tech manufacturing facility, among the best in the world, with the hope that a degree of learning can result as Malaysian workers are hired to work in the enterprise. Second, the investment of US$400 million represents a significant quantum of foreign investment. Third, the Malaysian market is also served by the textile products of the factory. Fourth, Malaysia does not have any

---

[98] Belt and Road Portal, 2016. International capacity cooperation. https://www.yidaiyilu.gov.cn/info/iList.jsp?tm_id=126&cat_id=10030&info_id=2175.

[99] The State Council of the People's Republic of China, 2015. Guideline of the State Council on promoting international cooperation in production capacity and equipment manufacturing. http://www.gov.cn/zhengce/content/2015-05/16/content_9771.htm.

domestic enterprises that can be undermined by competition from D&Y. Fifth, being locked into the Chinese industrial eco-system is no different from being part of other industrial systems. And, to the extent that China is more interested in popularising its own system than maximising profits, the terms negotiated between China and the host government may be more flexible than those negotiated with established multinationals from other countries. Finally, an area of direct benefit to Malaysia is D&Y's signing of an agreement with United Overseas Bank (Malaysia) Bhd (UOB) for credit financing services, settlement services and a range of comprehensive financial services, mainly for the purchase of land and for construction, as well as some trade financing.

On balance, then, this foreign investment should be considered as lending Malaysia a helping hand. However, for Malaysia, the extent of this help depends as much on its ability and willingness to take steps to upgrade its technological capabilities. This depends too on China's willingness, through its private but state-backed enterprise, to transfer the requisite technology through training. Moreover, there is much that is novel in this relationship between D&Y and the Malaysian state. First is the objective of the investment. Unlike other projects, it is not solely focused on the sale of products that is the primary concern of foreign manufactures. Instead, the focus of this investment is on the equipment and facilities that D&Y hopes Malaysian enterprises will acquire, locking them into the Chinese production system. Second, is the technological gap between D&Y and local capabilities, one that is so large that technology transfer cannot easily take place, making local sourcing difficult. Any training to close this gap may actually help to lock into the Chinese industrial eco-system. Finally, is the issue of the significance of the Chinese state. In this case, the high-tech equipment, together with all the technology accruing from it, comes from a state enterprise, although it is a private sector entity that is undertaking the investment. Although the source of fixed assets funding for this project is undisclosed, the likelihood is that it comes from state-owned banks.

B. *State Chinese Venture*

Case Study 6: CRRC Zhuzhou Locomotive Co. Ltd. (CRRC ZELC)
CRRC Corporation Limited (CRRC) is the world's largest supplier of rail transit equipment, with the most complete product lines and leading technologies. Its main businesses cover R&D, design, manufacture, repair,

sale, lease and technical services for rolling stock, urban rail transit vehicles, engineering machinery, all types of electrical equipment, electronic equipment and parts, electric products and environmental protection equipment, consulting services, industrial investment and management, asset management, import and export.[100] CRRC is one of 97 'yang qi'. Headquartered in Beijing, CRRC has 46 wholly-owned and majority-owned subsidiaries and over 180,000 employees.

Located in Hunan province, CRRC Zhuzhou Locomotive Co. Ltd. (CRRC ZELC) is the key subsidiary of CRRC.[101] In 2010, CRRC ZELC was awarded the order of 38 inter-city bullet trains in Malaysia, leading to the first export of China's electric traction bullet trains overseas. In order to solve the worries of local customers, in 2011, China's first overseas rail transit '4S' store, CRRC Kuala Lumpur Maintenance Sdn Bhd with investment by CRRC ZELC, was established in Kuala Lumpur.[102]

In April 2015, a subsidiary of CRRC ZELC, rail transport solution provider CRRC Rolling Stock Center (Malaysia) Sdn Bhd (CRRC CRM) was established.[103] With a total investment of approximately RMB400 million, CRRC ZELC began production at its first rolling stock plant outside China through CRRC CRM, at Batu Gajah, in the state of Perak. With a manufacturing base spanning 50-acres, its state-of-the-art manufacturing plant is responsible for a range of business operations involving rail transportation. This enterprise offers a one-stop rail solution combining production, welding, assembly, testing, overhaul and refurbishment for Electronic Locomotive, Diesel Locomotive, Electric Multiple Unit (EMU), Diesel Multiple Unit (DMU), Mass Rapid Transit (MRT), Light Rail Vehicle (LRV), High Speed Train (HST) and other rail transport equipment. CRRC CRM operated with an annual capacity

---

[100] CRRC Corporation Limited (CRRC), 2019. Company profile. http://www.crrcgc.cc/en/g5141.aspx.

[101] CRRC Zhuzhou Locomotive Co., Ltd. (CRRC ZELC), 2019. Company overview. https://www.crrcgc.cc/zjen/g2012.aspx.

[102] *chinanews.com*, 2017. CRRC ZELC strakes rooted in Malaysia: From 'stay' to 'guest' (in Chinese). https://www.chinanews.com/cj/2017/04-14/8199465.shtml.

[103] CRRC Zhuzhou Locomotive Co., Ltd. (CRRC ZELC), 2017. CRRC ZELC helps Malaysia to manufacture the train in local (Belt and Road Initiative & Win-Win Strategy). http://www.crrcgc.cc/zjen/g1733/s4283/t285409.aspx.

of 200 new carriages produced each year, while offering intermediate overhaul and maintenance of 150 vehicles.[104]

From its commencement in October 2015 to full operation in April 2017, CRRC CRM had completed successfully its first order comprising 20 six-car trains awarded in 2012 and second order comprising 30 six-car trains awarded in 2013 for the Rapid KL—a subsidiary of Prasarana Malaysia Bhd's Ampang Line of the LRT network in Kuala Lumpur.[105] Prasarana had ordered a total of 50 six-car trains from CRRC ZELC with 15 produced and 35 assembled at CRRC CRM to serve the LRT Ampang Line. It meant that the existing Ampang Line vehicle supplier ABB Daimler Benz Transportation (ADtranz) was replaced by CRRC ZELC.

In April 2017, CRRC ZELC and the Ministry of Transport of Malaysia signed the contract for the supply of 13 hybrid EMUs and 9 high-speed EMUs in Changsha City, Hunan Province. In August 2017, Prasarana announced the award of the Light Rail Vehicle (LRV) work package to a consortium comprising CRRC ZELC, Siemens Limited China and Tegap Dinamik Sdn Bhd for the 37 km Light Rail Transit Line 3 (LRT3) project linking Bandar Utama in Petaling Jaya to Klang. This consortium was to be responsible for the design, manufacture, supply, delivery, installation, testing and commissioning of 42 six-car LRVs for the LRT3 project valued at RM1.56 billion ringgit.[106] By August 2017, CRRC ZELC had been awarded contracts to supply trains to 10 projects in Malaysia.[107]

There is no evidence that CRRC ZELC's presence in Malaysia has local financing except for the LRT3 project in which this company has two local partners. CRRC ZELC is unlikely to face financial constraints since its parent company CRRC is a 'yang qi' and it is also publicly-listed. The

---

[104] Belt and Road Portal, 2019. Belt and Road projects—CRRC Rolling Stock Center. https://eng.yidaiyilu.gov.cn/zgzc.htm.

[105] Economic and Commercial Office of the Embassy of the People's Republic of China in Malaysia, 2016. The longest light rail line in Malaysia runs on Chinese locomotives. http://my.mofcom.gov.cn/article/sbhz/201607/20160701351637.shtml.

The Star Online, 22 August 2016. CRRC plans to expand ops in Perak. https://www.thestar.com.my/business/business-news/2016/08/22/crrc-plans-to-expand-ops-in-perak.

[106] Prasarana Malaysia Bhd, 2017. LRT3 Light Rail Vehicle (LRV) work package awarded. https://www.lrt3.com.my/2017/08/02/lrv/.

[107] *Nikkei Asian Review*, 2017. China group secures $364m train order in Malaysia. https://asia.nikkei.com/Business/China-group-secures-364m-train-order-in-Malaysia.

Chinese government must have played a crucial role in these financial-industrial linkages of the first and subsequent investments.

Awarding construction projects through direct negotiation has become a major controversy because of the lack of transparency and difficulty in determining if the lowest, or best, cost project was selected. For example, during the supply and commission search for LRT3's rolling stock, only the CRRC ZELC–Siemens–Tegap Dinamik consortium participated in the Prasarana-tendered bid.[108] Questions remain if other potential bidders pulled out because of CRRC ZELC's cost competitiveness or because of a lack of due process. This project was suspended by the Mahathir administration after the general election in 2018, when a change of government occurred. The project resumed in October 2019, but at a lower cost, by reducing the quantity to be purchased.

It is also not clear why Tegap Dinamik was selected as a joint-venture partner given that the company's business is in constructing residential and non-residential properties and not transport infrastructure. In particular, Tegap Dinamik's participation as a partner gives rise to several questions. First, in what ways can Tegap Dinamik add value to the construction of LRT3? Second, is there room for technology acquisition and transfer? Alternatively, is this a case of foreign companies maximising the chances of winning a tender bid by partnering with a well-connected domestic firm?

Records from Companies Commission of Malaysia (CCM) reveal that Tegap Dinamik and the well-connected and a publicly-listed Malton group co-own Memang Perkasa Sdn Bhd, a property development company that had been embroiled in a land dispute in Kuala Lumpur.[109] While these developments do not necessarily suggest malpractice in this project, the complex web of shared interests between firms closely-connected to political leaders is a matter of great concern from the perspective of governance. These connections coincide with high concentrations of 'state-state' and 'state-private' investments. Since these relationships might have an impact on how public projects are being awarded,

---

[108] A total of five companies had pre-qualified for the tender in May 2016, but only the CRRC Zhuzhou Locomotive Co Ltd–Siemens Limited China–Tegap Dinamik Sdn Bhd consortium submitted its bid when tenders closed in November 2016.

[109] *EdgeProp.my*, 2018. Developer looks set to go ahead with project at Taman Rimba Kiara. https://www.edgeprop.my/content/1351235/developer-looks-set-go-ahead-project-taman-rimba-kiara.

there is a need to scrutinise existing and future investments and enhance transparency.

Servicing and maintenance projects for the Ampang Line was first awarded after direct negotiations between Keretapi Tanah Melayu Bhd (KTMB) and CRRC ZELC. Following this award, CRRC ZELC formed a joint-venture with a local firm to fulfil the contract. This partnership was needed because, according to CRRC ZELC, KTMB had poor train maintenance practices, leading to faster depreciation rates. Furthermore, the previous government did not want to sign an agreement with CRRC ZELC, despite public safety and reputational concerns.

According to the 'Guideline of the State Council on Promoting International Cooperation in Production Capacity and Equipment Manufacturing', the Chinese government is accelerating the 'going out' of 'advantageous' production capacity, so as to promote the 'going out' of equipment, technology, standards and services. Railway is one key industry that China has encouraged to establish assembly, maintenance bases and R&D centers in key countries where conditions permit.[110] As an SOE, CRRC ZELC was spurred by the central government to go out in accordance with the national strategy.[111]

CRRC ZELC was clearly eyeing business opportunities in the ASEAN market, with the company well-positioned to meet the next wave of demand for railway infrastructure in the region as well as in Malaysia. CRRC ZELC's vision is to make Malaysia a regional hub for the railway industry in Southeast Asia. Concerning manufacturing rolling stock, the Malaysian market alone appears too small for it to be economically viable. However, CRRC ZELC's vision to make Malaysia a regional hub for the railway industry in ASEAN presents an opportunity for technology acquisition and transfer, to meet the country's aspirations for technology-led growth. For Malaysia, more employment would be created, some upgrading of maintenance skills can be expected, while local vendors might be hired and through training and learning-by doing an overall upgrade in skills can be realised. CRRC ZELC's three subsidiaries in Malaysia employed about 80% locals. The company stated that it is guided by its vision to make Malaysia a regional hub for train manufacturing.

---

[110] The State Council of the People's Republic of China, 2015. Guideline of the State Council on promoting international cooperation in production capacity and equipment manufacturing. http://www.gov.cn/zhengce/content/2015-05/16/content_9771.htm.

[111] Interview with a staff of CRRC ZELC on December 2019.

The top management is committed to hiring Malaysians, initially, to staff assembly lines. In the near future, Malaysians are expected to assume positions in R&D and senior management. CRRC ZELC's strategy is also to be cost efficient—it is less expensive to hire locals than to pay Chinese expatriates.

However, this objective is hampered by a shortage of skilled Malaysian workers. This challenge has increased the recruitment period because CRRC ZELC has to send local staff for professional development and skills training in China. Moreover, CRRC ZELC has formed a partnership with local universities to train skilled workers. From CRRC ZELC's view, these efforts should remedy Malaysia's lack of specialists in railroad infrastructure.

On the other hand, CRRC ZELC envisages more engagement with the local SMEs to become better suppliers of spare parts. By training its suppliers so that they can produce more reliable parts and components, CRRC ZELC forms backward linkages that nurture a more competitive and diverse market ecosystem. This close supplier-buyer relationship is also consistent with the Malaysian government's objective to develop competitive manufacturers of components or services, usually SME entrepreneurs, for the domestic and global markets through the Vendor Development Programme (VDP). Apart from SMEs from Proton, the national car-maker, most of the VDP participants are found to have suboptimal partnerships with anchor companies. The VDP has been subjected to political interference, with well-connected SMEs protected by cosy contracts to the point that they are unwilling to expand and go global. These challenges have resulted in an SME sector that lacks innovation and technology upgrading.

As a beneficiary of direct negotiations, CRRC ZELC is part of the previous government's rent-seeking activities that hurt the economy. To the extent that CRRC's size and experience might have won it the contract even if an open tender was done, the damage caused by its selection is difficult to estimate. Yet, by being complicit in the previous government's questionable business practices, the company has possibly exposed Malaysia to financial risks, the scale of which is only now coming to light.

The Asian Development Bank (ADB) estimates that by 2030, ASEAN needs between US$2.8 trillion and US$3.1 trillion of total infrastructure investment.[112] According to the same report, investment needs for rail transport beyond 2020 in the Greater Mekong Sub-region stands at US$30.1 billion, three times the amount that is needed in Central Asia. As multinational companies step up their investments in ASEAN's infrastructure development, Malaysia should leverage on globally competitive firms such as CRRC ZELC to expand regionally. By facilitating technology transfer and know-how, Malaysia can become a net exporter of (Chinese) transportation infrastructure and services to the region.

CRRC ZELC's plant is built on a 30-year lease with the Perak state government. When this lease ends, the government can decide whether to reclaim the land or allow CRRC ZELC to continue to operate. Until then, the question of CRRC ZELC's share of benefits from its Southeast Asian project can only be partially answered.

From product export, local servicing and maintenance, and from local assembly to local production, the project should represent the upgrading process of China-Malaysia economic relations. China's products and services, as well as its investments and technologies are exported to Malaysia. Greenfield investments, especially productive investments of this kind, can potentially create and nurture a new industry and aid in creating a sustainable industrial ecosystem. The case of CRRC ZELC in making Malaysia the regional hub in rolling-stock manufacturing can be an example for attracting more investors, thereby propelling Malaysia into new markets and creating new sources of economic growth.

Simply attracting foreign investments for short-term gains can have a positive bearing on a recovering economy. However, the bigger challenge is how to achieve substantial and sustainable outcomes by tapping into China's investments for Malaysia's own development. It is best to acquire the core technology that has been willingly transferred and add value to improve the level of the Malaysian industries by a few channels. First, Malaysian enterprises, that is the GLCs and SMEs, should not limit technology transfer to purchasing equipment with provisions for training of technicians to manage and operate them. Malaysian staff need also to participate in localised R&D processes. Second, Malaysian enterprises should consider investing in joint-ventures which will allow

---

[112] Asian Development Bank (ADB), 2017. *Meeting Asia's infrastructure needs*. Mandaluyong City, Philippines: Asian Development Bank.

them to import technology and acquaint themselves in its use. Finally, Chinese manufacturing companies cultivating local suppliers in producing core and other components are another source of technology transfer.

C. State-Private Chinese Venture

Case Study 7: Alliance Steel (M) Sdn Bhd
The integrated steel project by Alliance Steel in the Malaysia-China Kuantan Industrial Park (MCKIP), with a production capacity of 3.5 million tons of steel per annum, is the first as well as the key project in this industrial park. As a leading enterprise in the MCKIP, Alliance Steel must be considered an outcome of the BRI. As indicated earlier, a twin project to the MCKIP, the China-Malaysia Qinzhou Industrial Park, is located in Qinzhou City. Both industrial parks have been designated as key nodes of the BRI's Maritime Silk Road. Alliance Steel's Malaysia venture also constitutes part of China's 'going out' strategy, since it is in a key enterprise in the manufacturing sector.

Resource-seeking was clearly not a motive for Alliance Steel's entry into Malaysia. As with other Malaysian steel plants, the raw material, iron ore, is imported from Australia, Indonesia and Canada.[113] One possible reason for this project was the implementation of China's policy to transfer its technology, an important aspect of its foreign investment planning.[114] China sees market potential in Malaysia for the application of Alliance Steel's technology, to test outcomes in its technology transfer. Moreover, if this potential is fulfilled, it will lock the Malaysian steel sector into China's industrial eco-system for steel production.

The offshoring of steel production from China can conceivably be an outcome of wage pressures or competition within that country. And, it could mark the beginning of a new international supply chain for the Chinese steel industry, as Alliance Steel's products are to be exported to China as well as the rest of Southeast Asia.

Further, with the emergence of the China-US trade war and the anti-dumping policy implemented by many other countries, Alliance Steel can take advantage of Malaysia's regional trade preferential policies to export.

---

[113] Interview with a staff of Alliance Steel on December 2018.

[114] See the 'Guideline of the State Council on Promoting International Cooperation in Production Capacity and Equipment Manufacturing' for further information on this (http://www.gov.cn/zhengce/content/2015-05/16/content_9771.htm).

In addition, its products should meet domestic demand for steel from mega infrastructure projects in Malaysia, such as the ECRL. These big infrastructure projects are expected to consume the most steel, while it is presumed that the needs of the domestic real estate and construction sector are to be met by Malaysian producers. Therefore, the competition that Malaysian producers will encounter with the presence of Alliance Steel is expected to be limited, although these presumptions may not be borne out.

Alliance Steel (M) Sdn Bhd was established in April 2014 with total investment of US$1.4 billion.[115] It is a state-private-joint-stock enterprise, with joint investments by Guangxi Beibu Gulf Port International Group Co. Ltd. (GBG), a large provincial state-owned enterprise directly under the government of Guangxi Autonomous Region,[116] and Guangxi Shenglong Metallurgical (GSM) Co. Ltd.,[117] a private joint-stock enterprise.[118] This project is GBG's first overseas investment under its 'mixed ownership' mode. This investment also appears to be the province's response to the call for mixed-ownership reform of China's state enterprises.[119] The professional operation of this steel project is handled by GSM. Steve Hu of GSM was selected to head this overseas joint-venture enterprise. That GSM was tasked to head Alliance Steel was probably because GBG was not initially in the steel business, but GBG soon realised that without its support, the private enterprise GSM would have no access to bank financing. This compelled GBG to enter into a joint-venture with GSM, which would lend its weight as a state enterprise to secure bank financing.[120]

---

[115] Alliance Steel (M) Sdn Bhd, 2019. Launching of syndicated loan withdrawal procedure for 3.5 million tons of integrated steel project. http://alliancesteel.com.my/article_33.html?lang=zh.

[116] Beibu Gulf Port Group, 2019. Group profile. http://www.bbwgw.com/cms/category/23.dhtml.

[117] Alliance Steel (M) Sdn Bhd, 2019. Company profile. http://alliancesteel.com.my/articleList_6_1.html.

[118] Guangxi Shenglong Metallurgical Co. Ltd., 2019. Brief introduction of Guangxi Shenglong Metallurgical Co. Ltd. http://www.gxslyj.com/about.aspx?ParentId=2&BaseInfoCateId=9&CateId=9.

[119] The State-owned Assets Supervision and Administration, 2017. When the state enterprise reform began, the first shot' of mix-ownership was adopted. http://www.sasac.gov.cn/n2588025/n2588139/c2822453/content.html.

[120] Interview with a staff of GBG on November 2019.

Although classified as a private enterprise, Alliance Steel is a good example of the murky definition of a Chinese private enterprise. While it has partial state ownership, thereby enabling it to qualify for funding from the Chinese banks, management of Alliance Steel is in the hands of the private partner.

Alliance Steel is a key project for achieving international capacity cooperation between China and MCKIP. Using an advanced alternating current electric arc furnace and long process technology from China, Alliance Steel is expected to have substantial cost advantages when fully operational. The Malaysian government clearly sees this technology, not available in the country, as having the potential to displace domestic small-scale steel mills that are saddled with high energy consumption, high production cost and low output. This technology has the potential to accelerate technological development of the Malaysian steel industry, if well implemented.

China Construction Bank, Export-Import Bank of China and Agricultural Bank of China formed a project syndicate to provide financing of US$664 million and RMB2 billion[121] for this project. China Construction Bank and Export-Import Bank were the joint lead banks of this syndicate, with China Construction Bank taking on an additional role as loan and settlement agent. This financing model is also a first for Chinese foreign investment. The China Construction Bank, the Export-Import Bank of China and the Agricultural Bank of China, all state-owned financial institutions, pioneered the cross-border syndicated direct lending model for this project. China Import and Export Credit Insurance is providing professional overseas investment insurance services for the project. This insurance enterprise is responsible for providing efficient and high-quality financial service for companies in Guangxi intending to invest overseas, with Alliance Steel being a good example of what is on offer.

Since funding for the entire investment comes from Chinese banks, this ensures adequacy of capital for this project. This mode of financing also indicates that China has a variety of institutional sources, from commercial banks to designated policy banks, to offer project funding. These sources of funding are available even when only SOEs are involved.

---

[121] RMB2 billion was approximately equal to US$297 million, according to the exchange rate in October 2016. This meant that the total financing was about US$1 billion.

This integrated steel project was designed by CISDI Engineering Co. Ltd. and constructed by Shanghai Baoye Group Corp. Ltd., China 19th Metallurgical Corporation, China 22MCC Group Corporation Ltd. and Sinosteel Corporation.[122] Apart from Sinosteel Corporation, all these enterprises are subsidiaries of China Metallurgical Group Corporation, which is an SOE directly under the central government. Sinosteel Corporation is an SOE under the State-owned Assets Supervision and Administration Commission of the State Council (SASAC).[123] These Chinese SOEs and their subsidiaries were put in charge from project design, purchase of equipment, construction, geological survey to project management. Chinese workers were brought in for the plant's construction, irking many Malaysians but this was justified by the project managers on the basis of speed as they completed their work ahead of schedule.

On 17 May 2018, the pilot production ceremony of the No. 1 blast furnace of the integrated steel project, designed and equipped by CISDI Engineering, was held on the platform of the iron field.[124] CISDI Engineering was the whole industrial chain service provider for this steel project. It had won the contract for overall plant and engineering and other designs, together with complete sets of equipment and raw materials, as well as continuous casting blast furnace design.[125] CISDI Engineering also undertook the task of whole-system procurement management and equipment management of steel mills, while also providing high-end consulting services to enhance the competitiveness of the project. It is the most important participating enterprise in this joint steel project.[126]

---

[122] Alliance Steel (M) Sdn Bhd, 2018. Company profile. http://cn.alliancesteel.com.my/lggk.

[123] Sinosteel Group Corporation Limited, 2019. http://en.sinosteel.com/col/col308/index.html.

[124] CISDI Group Co. Ltd., 2018. Group Profile. The commissioning ceremony of no.1 blast furnace of CISDI Kuantan Alliance Steel is held ceremoniously. http://www.cisdigroup.com.cn/html/mtzx/gsdt/18/05/2017.html.

[125] These contracting arrangements showcased the strength of CISDI Engineering in the field of steel engineering technology, engineering solutions, complete sets of equipment, steel design, equipment manufacturing, automation control and system integration.

[126] Sohu Media Platform, 2018. Ignition of No. 1 blast furnace of CISDI's Malaysian Alliance Steel. http://m.sohu.com/n/540074838/.

Other enterprises, all state-owned subsidiaries, had, however, other vital roles. Hunan Hetian Engineering Project Management Co. Ltd., a subsidiary of China Metallurgical Group Corporation, provided whole process project management services.[127] Wuhan Surveying-geotechnical Research Institute Co. Ltd., also a subsidiary of China Metallurgical Group Corporation, was responsible for the geological survey project of the whole plant. Its project department had to overcome many difficulties, such as complicated equipment procurement, personnel visa issues, hot weather and heavy-duty tasks. To their credit, they completed in 75 days the key tasks that took the local survey team two years to complete, thereby reducing considerably the construction period. Further savings were achieved when the drilling depth and layout were optimized, all without compromising project safety.[128]

After several rounds of bidding, Sinopec Lubricant Company won the bid from among many international brands to become the largest oil supplier and partner of Alliance Steel.[129] Sinopec Lubricant Company is a subsidiary of China Petroleum and Chemical Corporation (Sinopec), a central SOE.

As a greenfield investment, the Alliance Steel project represents a much-needed injection of foreign capital, since the entire sum is financed in China and invested in Malaysia. Since Chinese SOEs are heavily involved in all aspects of Alliance Steel's operation, they are also sources of funding for this project. With respect to the transfer of knowledge, the gap between the technology of Alliance Steel and Malaysian steel plants is extremely large. Even with training, it will take time for Malaysian enterprises to catch up with Alliance Steel's technology. The best that can be hoped for in the short term is some tacit learning that will enable Malaysian workers to familiarise themselves with the use of the equipment. The responsibility for accelerating the learning process lies less with

---

[127] Hunan Hetian Engineering Project Management Co. Ltd., 2016. The construction mobilisation meeting of 350 tons steel project and the commencement ceremony of 2×1080m cubed blast furnace project were held ceremonially. http://www.hunanhetian.com/viewer.aspx?c=3&m=14&i=257.

[128] Wuhan Surveying-geotechnical Research Institute Co. Ltd. of MCC, 2016. Wuhan Surveying-geotechnical Research Institute Co., Ltd. of MCC received a letter of thanks from Alliance Steel. http://www.wsgri.com/wsgrimobile/qywh75/gsdt4/305197/index.html.

[129] Sinopec Lubricant Company, 2019. Sinopec Lubricant Company behind the Belt and Road Initiative. http://www.sinolube.com/content/details66_32962.html.

the government securing technology transfer terms and with Malaysia's ability to upgrade its technology to narrow this gap with China. The sooner this ability is acquired, the better will Malaysian firms be able to secure participation in parts of the value chain for steel manufacturing.

Technological constraints at the Malaysian end may limit the benefits that can be derived in the short-term. On the other hand, substantial investment funds were provided to an enterprise that is technologically advanced, export-oriented, employed local workers and could potentially be part of a domestic steel supply chain. Alliance Steel's location at the MCKIP is helpful for the development of this massive industrial park. While fiscal incentives such as tax exemptions were provided by the Malaysian government,[130] Alliance Steel constitutes a major component of the ECER, which serves to industrialise under-developed states on the east coast of the peninsula.

Despite this, much criticism of the Alliance Steel project has been expressed by Malaysian stakeholders. The extensive role played by Chinese enterprises in this project has led to unhappiness about Alliance Steel being more beneficial to China at the expense of Malaysia. Complaints have been voiced about the use of Chinese labour during and after construction of the plant. Concerns have been raised of the inability of Malaysian steel companies to compete with Alliance Steel, given the latter's technological depth. There have also been criticisms about China dumping excess capacity in Malaysia.

With respect to Chinese labour, the presence of Chinese workers during the construction of the plant was a source of complaint by locals. However, by the time the plant was fully operational, it was reported that the company employed some 1200 Malaysians and only 200 Chinese.[131] In a more recent statement, Alliance Steel's management stated: 'Presently, we have about 1000 Chinese staff and 2600 Malaysians. We want to hire another 1000 locals. How fast can the Chinese workers be replaced by locals will depend on how fast Malaysians can acquire the skill via our transfer of technology programs. However, for the construction of furnaces and other high-technology work, the company had to bring in China's specialists.' The company also noted that Malaysians

---

[130] MIDA approved the incentives.

[131] *Malaysiakini*, 18 April 2018. MCKIP not closed to local workers, says Malay business group. https://www.malaysiakini.com/news/420477.

had benefited by getting about RM1 billion worth of construction work from Alliance Steel. At full production capacity, Alliance Steel is expected to contribute about 7.0 million tons of cargo throughput annually for Kuantan Port. As a result, Kuantan Port will see a jump in its revenue.

On competition with Malaysian steel companies, three local steelmakers currently use blast furnaces: Ann Joo, Eastern Steel and Alliance Steel. The blast furnaces of Ann Joo and Eastern Steel are 450 m^3 and 600 m^3 respectively, while Alliance Steel currently has two 1080 m^3 blast furnaces. In terms of production capacity, Alliance Steel mainly produces bar rods, wire rods, H-beams and billets, with an annual designed output of 3.5 million tons.[132] The current output has reached about 80% of the designed capacity output.[133] By way of comparison, the annual production capacities of the four Malaysian steel firms are: Lion Industries, 2.68 million tons; Southern Steel, 1.65 million tons; Ann Joo, 0.70 million tons; and Masteel, 0.45 million tons. Clearly, in terms of blast furnace volume and design capacity, the scale of Alliance Steel far exceeds those of the Malaysian mills.

More pertinent to competition with domestic firms, Alliance Steel has promised the Malaysian government that most of its long steel (bar rods and wire rods) will be exported, with only about 30%, or 450,000 tons, sold domestically. At present, Malaysia's national demand for long steel is about 6.13 million tons a year, with the four local long steel companies supplying only about 3.48 million tons. Even with the 450,000 tons of domestic sales of Alliance Steel, there is still a big supply gap that remains to be filled. Indeed, Alliance Steel could well play a positive role in helping meet Malaysia's supply shortfalls.

One concrete example is the H-beam, a type of section steel. Alliance Steel has an annual output of about two million tons of H-beams, all of which will be entirely exported. Moreover, since no steel company in Malaysia produces H-beams, the influence of Alliance Steel on the overall

---

[132] RH Research, 2018. Latest developments of Alliance Steel. https://www.facebook.com/rhresearch/posts/2083381961673412/.

[133] Interview with a staff of Alliance Steel on December 2018.

domestic steel industry is minimal.¹³⁴ There is currently very limited local demand for high-end steel products such as the H-beam.¹³⁵

With respect to China dumping obsolete equipment, Alliance Steel's equipment is extremely advanced and novel. There is little basis for claims that refurbished machinery and equipment from plants in China are being shut down and are being shipped to Malaysia.¹³⁶

Far from having a negative impact, the location and operation of the Alliance Steel plant has a number of positive implications. First, the location of the plant is next to a port. Crucially too, the location of the port is very strategic. With high enough local content, the steel produced by Alliance Steel can also qualify for the ASEAN Free Trade Area agreement and avoid import duties.¹³⁷ In future, Alliance Steel could compete with Chinese steel imports. If this occurs, Alliance Steel might be able to displace some of the two million tons of Chinese steel imports each year.

The model personified by Alliance Steel is more accurately characterised as one based on decision-making by a Chinese hybrid enterprise with a Malaysian state authority without adequately consulting other stakeholders such as private industry. For Alliance Steel, this model appears to be one from which it derives much benefit, with China being able to claim success in its attempt to implement the BRI as well as publicise its technology. China also hopes to get the Malaysian steel industry to use Chinese equipment for steel production. Malaysians get to learn from more advanced technology than what they are using, secure employment at the mill, and potentially be a competitive exporter of steel products.

---

¹³⁴ Alex Investment Review, 2018 Can Malaysian steel companies make steady moy in the future? https://xxscyehxx.blogspot.com/2018/01/blog-post.html?m=1&fbclid=IwAR2XwQew7pXlxFaOYHWhfCRTJ6yhClfx2glKe7IP1C_QWdp5ACLRJ7LcuXA.

¹³⁵ Interview with a staff of Alliance Steel on December 2018.

¹³⁶ Interview with a staff of Alliance Steel on December 2018. The allegation was these plants in China were being shut down as they were loss-making concerns.

¹³⁷ *The Edge*, 2015. Shake-up for local steel makers. https://www.theedgemarkets.com/article/shake-local-steel-makers?type=From%20The%20Edge.

CHAPTER 4

Analysing Chinese Investments in Malaysia

KEY FEATURES OF THE SEVEN CASES

Table 4.1 draws out the key features of the seven studies under review. Specific attention is drawn to the institutional architecture under which these projects function and the financial-industrial linkages that have been created, to identify the key funders of these ventures. In these early-stage high-risk ventures, though with extremely high potential economic outcomes, sources of funding are important. Table 4.1 also reviews the role of the state, including where decision-making power is situated in each of these ventures and if it functions in a helping hand, invisible hand or grabbing hand manner or a combination of these hands.

The production networks that prevail are reviewed in this table, to draw attention to how links are forged between Chinese enterprises and Malaysian firms, SMEs in particular. Table 4.1 also offers information on the outcomes, including the projected ones, of these seven projects, as well as their impact on the development objectives of the Malaysian government. The form of state-business relation (SBR) employed in each project is assessed in Table 4.1, to point out the differences and similarities in ventures that are state-state, state-private, private-private and private in nature.

Table 4.1 indicates that a variety of institutional collaborations have been forged, indicating also the rather diverse arrangements that characterise Chinese foreign investments. These diverse forms of fund flows are not captured in mainstream Western theories of foreign investments

Table 4.1 Summary of the seven cases

First section: Joint ventures

Name of company	Financial-industrial linkages	Institutional architecture	Outcomes of project (including expected ones)	Impact on Malaysia's enterprise and economic development objectives
Proton (Chinese private with Malaysian private)—automobile production	• Proton received substantial financial and non-financial support (in the form of grants) from the Malaysian state for its development, due to its national car status and support from Mahathir Mohamad • After Proton was sold to DRB-HICOM, it continued to receive state support, as in the soft loan given to it to offset its losses • Post-sale to Geely, Proton has most likely used internal funding and local loans to finance the first phase of the expansion of its Tanjung Malim plant • Funding for development of Proton: it took a loan in 2019 from a Chinese bank for R&D and infrastructure development	• Proton's national car status and its backing by Mahathir meant that the state had a substantial say in the development of this project, even after it was sold to DRB-HICOM • When Geely obtained an equity stake in Proton, the state essentially relinquished control over the national car project's development to a foreign-owned enterprise from China, now a key technology supplier in this new institutional framework • The development of Proton is now determined by profitability, domestic and foreign market share and the technology provided by Geely • Proton's choice of technology partner was guided by the criteria stipulated by the government, based on a soft loan given to the company in 2016 (despite its private status)	• Proton and Geely are both profit-motivated • The objectives of both companies match in terms of expansion in domestic and foreign markets • Remains to be seen if Proton-Geely can penetrate the Japanese-dominated Southeast Asian auto market • Still uncertain if Proton can move from centre of excellence to design centre	• Local sourcing will be based on the transformed vendor development system • Vendors have to invest to upgrade themselves technologically and reduce costs • The upgraded vendors will come from a second round of investments between selected vendors and Chinese suppliers from China, for upgrading and cost-cutting and to penetrate the export market • Positive, but unclear whether new car designs in Malaysia by Malaysians can be achieved in the long-term

First section: Joint ventures

Name of company	Financial-industrial linkages	Institutional architecture	Outcomes of project (including expected ones)	Impact on Malaysia's enterprise and economic development objectives
		• The state played the role of helping hand • Geely's choice of Proton was to use it to enter the Southeast Asian market • Vendor development under Geely: matching of domestic and Chinese vendors—additional investments from China, collaborations on supply chain to meet international standards with the intention to also export Chinese parts and components		
MCKIP (Chinese state with Malaysian GLC)—industrial park development	• The national status of the park was why state support was offered. The federal government provided for infrastructure development, such as roads to connect the Park to the Kuantan port • In terms of financing the development of the Park, there is no direct information, but it can be inferred that the Chinese SOE took a loan from an SOE bank to finance the project	• The location of this Park is in the ECER. The area was selected for the development of the Park due to its location, specifically in the home state of then Prime Minister Najib Razak • MCKIP is to be developed synergistically with Kuantan Port. The development of the Park and Kuantan Port is to be undertaken by the same partnership, comprising IJM and Guangxi Beibu	• Immediate goal is securing foreign investment and generating employment • Employment creation is used as an indicator of its economic benefits to the nation	• Since the development of the Park is conducted through an intermediary (even though a GLC) which is only interested in making profits, long-term development goals of the country are not taken into explicit account in the conduct of the Park's development

(continued)

Table 4.1 (continued)

First section: Joint ventures

Name of company	Financial-industrial linkages	Institutional architecture	Outcomes of project (including expected ones)	Impact on Malaysia's enterprise and economic development objectives
	• IJM finances the project's development ventures through bonds, term loans, revolving credit and other borrowings as it is a listed company, rather than depending on development banks • There is no reported information that IJM took a loan from China. Unlikely, as this would have been queried by shareholders • Later, IJM switched the source of its domestic loan (in ringgit) from Maybank to a Chinese SOE bank branch, CCB (M), due to lower interest rates offered	• IJM is a construction company, with no expertise in foreign investment promotion. IJM therefore left it to the Chinese partner to promote the Park in China and bring in investors, based on its networks in China • The project is under the control of the Chinese state, through its SOE and SOE banks • Investments reflect China's interests, i.e. the export of industries according to China's mandate • IJM plays an intermediary role. IJM has to secure investment approval and tax incentives, as well as acquire land • The state, in the form of the GLC (IJM), plays the role of helping hand	• Malaysian partner depends on Chinese partner to draw in investors • Malaysian partner takes care of local issues such as land, approvals and incentives and its own bottom line as it is accountable to its shareholders for its investments and loans	• State institutions for SME development, such as SME Corp, are not involved in fostering the development of SMEs via linkages with Park's manufacturers • Local sourcing, in terms of intermediate inputs, remains to be seen as it is directed by market forces, i.e. it depends on costs, etc. • Technology transfer through domestic sourcing is unlikely to happen for reasons of scale. It is difficult for Malaysian SMEs to compete against Chinese suppliers for reasons of scale and technology gap

First section: Joint ventures

Name of company	Financial-industrial linkages	Institutional architecture	Outcomes of project (including expected ones)	Impact on Malaysia's enterprise and economic development objectives
DFTZ Phase 2: Alibaba's e-commerce hub (services) for ASEAN (Chinese private with Malaysian GLC)	• Although the DFTZ is a national initiative, the first phase was funded by the Najib administration was funded by Pos Malaysia, which was a former GLC, sold to Syed Mokhtar Albukhary (he also owns DRB-HICOM, linked to Geely and the Proton project) • The second phase was developed by Cainiao and MHAB. No reported loans from China for this project. Alibaba and MAHB have the reserves to fund the development of this e-commerce hub	• Facilities at the hub are being developed by MAHB • This joint-venture appears to be dependent on Alibaba to create demand for the facilities at the e-commerce hub, via its businesses and corporate partners • Malaysian partner, MAHB, plays similar role as IJM in the MCKIP, i.e. to get the land and approvals from local authorities, as well as access to state incentives • Although the project is state-driven, the operations are determined by a GLC, which is profit motivated, while Alibaba's focus is on profit-making and securing access to regional markets • State plays the role of helping hand	• Immediate goal is utilisation of facilities for e-commerce activities • Employment creation is used as an indicator of its economic benefits to Malaysia • No development agenda • Malaysian partner depends on Chinese partner to create demand for the facilities developed at the e-commerce hub • Malaysian partner takes care of local issues such as land, approvals and incentives	• Malaysian partner is not concerned about SMEs being able to export • Only concern is air cargo and air traffic and the utilisation of its airports and facilities • Malaysian sources of services needed at the hub are not a priority in the e-commerce plans. • Government objective is to help SMEs to export—note, this is a completely different focus from promoting manufacturing activities

(continued)

Table 4.1 (continued)

Second section: Chinese firms (sole ownership)

Name of company	Financial-industrial linkages	Institutional architecture	Outcomes of project (projected)	Impact on Malaysia's development objectives
Jinko (Chinese private only; listed in New York)—solar cells and module production	• There is no state support in terms of financing the development of Jinko since this is a foreign investment-based project • Took a loan from Maybank, a Malaysian GLC	• Facilitated by Penang state government and MIDA, with shared interests in attracting FDI and increasing employment • Role of MIDA and Penang state: Eased bureaucracy and to provide incentives • Role of Malaysian state: the Penang government and the federal institution, MIDA, facilitated Jinko's entry, as with other FDI in manufacturing • State plays role of helping hand	• Meets Malaysia's plan to develop a solar ecosystem with foreign investment and incentives for foreign investors • Profit-centred • Production as well as R&D to improve process efficiency for competitive reasons—focus on process technology transfer • Re-investment for new product production • Development of new products are conducted outside Malaysia • Continuation of production in Malaysia to be exported to new company established in the United States due to US-China trade conflict in 2019 • Expansion of R&D facility in Penang in December 2019. To shift beyond cost reduction. R&D in line with changes in Jinko and possible global realignment due to the trade war	• Contributed to Malaysia becoming world's third largest exporter of solar panels • Environmental impact depends on monitoring for compliance • Local sourcing of components not reported at all • Positive but unclear whether new product design in Malaysia by Malaysians can be achieved in the long-term

Second section: Chinese firms (sole ownership)

Name of company	Financial-industrial linkages	Institutional architecture	Outcomes of project (projected)	Impact on Malaysia's development objectives
D&Y Textile (Chinese private only; reformed, as it once functioned as an SOE)—textiles	• No local funding for FDI. All fixed assets funding sourced from China • Closely related to state enterprises • However, agreement signed with UOB for land acquisition, and construction, as well as some trade financing	• D&Y's choice of Malaysia is based on lower cost of raw materials and energy (than in China), robust infrastructure, good export facilities, good bilateral relations • D&Y to help China Hi-Tech to build demonstration base of its equipment in Malaysia • For Malaysia, D&Y is expected to anchor a high-tech textile industrial park and upgrade existing textile sector	• Greenfield foreign direct investment brought in US$200 million to Malaysia • Generates employment in Johor state • Projected foreign exchange earnings of US$350 million • Can take advantage of Malaysia's regional trading connections, including intended membership of TPP. China's firms can use Malaysia as export platform to third countries • Strengthen competitiveness in a maturing industry, but potential lock into Chinese equipment and industrial eco-system • Industrial upgrading through training, but Malaysia needs to raise its game in technology education • Participation in textile supply chain	• Meets objective of revitalising the mature textile sector • Strengthen role as competitive exporter • Has objective of technology upgrade. However, achievement of objective depends on Malaysia's technological capabilities • No competition with Malaysian textile companies

(continued)

82   E. T. GOMEZ ET AL.

Table 4.1 (continued)

Second section: Chinese firms (sole ownership)

Name of company	Financial-industrial linkages	Institutional architecture	Outcomes of project (projected)	Impact on Malaysia's development objectives
CRRC ZELC (Chinese state only; subsequent projects have local GLC and private partners)—Rail transit equipment	• No Malaysian funding, except for LRT3 project with two partners • No funding constraint. CRRC is 'yang qi' • Chinese government plays crucial role in first and subsequent investments	• Chinese state retained structural power • As world's largest rail transit equipment supplier with most complete product lines and technologies, it should be globally competitive • But rolling stock contract awarded through much criticised direct negotiation • Such 'state-state' contracts raise questions about transparent governance • Service and maintenance contract for Ampang Line awarded to CRRC ZELC through direct negotiation	• Employment of Malaysians first for assembly line, then R&D and management • But shortage of skilled Malaysian workers. In the interim, training in China, and partnerships with Malaysian universities • Also hampered by SMEs lacking innovation, while vendor programme driven by political influence • CRRC ZELC unhappy it is treated as a foreign company by MoF's Technology Depository Agency • Both 'grabbing' and 'helping' hands of state are present. Contracts from direct negotiations indicate the grabbing hand, but training and R&D represent helping hand	• CRRC's plan to use Malaysia as a launchpad to Southeast Asia. In line with Malaysia's development objectives, greenfield investment has potential for creation of industrial ecosystem, based on Chinese technology • Revive Malaysia's manufacturing sector • Promote SME vendor programme

Second section: Chinese firms (sole ownership)

Name of company	Financial-industrial linkages	Institutional architecture	Outcomes of project (projected)	Impact on Malaysia's development objectives
Alliance Steel (Chinese state and private joint venture)—Steel production	• No Malaysian funding. All funding sourced from China, i.e. China Construction Bank, Export-Import Bank (joint lead banks) and Agricultural Bank of China • These three SOE banks pioneered cross-border syndicated direct lending model for the project	• Chinese state retained structural power • Fully-owned by China. All construction work and supplies by Chinese companies • May mark beginning of new supply chain, ending back in China • A key enterprise in MCKIP • ECER promoted and MIDA approved • Location to take advantage of Malaysia's regional trade preferential policies	• During construction phase, all Chinese workers • Malaysian workers when fully operational—2000 jobs • Technology gap large, takes time to transfer. Short-term training to use equipment only • Limited competition with Malaysian mills. Alliance's capacity far larger, most output exported • Machinery is high-tech, not dumping sort • Location is strategic. Next to port, can qualify for ASEAN-FTA • Although state-state project carries risk of rent expropriation, Alliance Steel has on balance provided Malaysia with a helping hand	• Meets the objective of developing high-tech export sector in the long run • Can substitute for steel imports, including from China • Facilitate upgrading of local steel industry • Provides employment in short-term

Source Compiled by authors

which are primarily private sector-based. The nature of these SBRs underscore the complexity of the Chinese concept of the 'state', with its considerable overlaps with what should be termed as the 'non-state' rather than the 'private' sector. How specific forms of SBRs shape particular systems of production networks are also appraised to determine the outcomes of these seven projects on the Malaysian economy.

A further feature of these case studies relates to the issue of technology transfer from China. While Western multinationals have expressed concern about technology theft arising from foreign investments, enterprises from China appear less concerned about host countries acquiring Chinese technology. Indeed, China's 'going out' policy explicitly stresses the need to export Chinese technology. This is well-illustrated in several of the case studies. Such a policy affords opportunities to Malaysian SMEs to acquire technology that comes with foreign investments. However, it also demands a high level of human capital that is able to successfully adopt and apply this technology. As is obvious in the case studies, Malaysia does not have the requisite human capital to benefit from this sort of technology transfer.

Case Studies: Key Findings

What emerges from this review of the seven case studies is that the Malaysian government does not have in place a clear policy direction to determine how industrial and high-tech-based projects are to be fashioned, even with the promise of greenfield-based foreign investments. This is the case even though the role of the states of Malaysia and China in creating these ventures is quite evident. While SOEs and GLCs figure well in these projects in the manufacturing and services sectors, there was a clear endeavour by the states of Malaysia and China to allow for the involvement of private enterprises. In these ventures, the presence of large-scale privately-owned firms from China is evident, while in Malaysia the government aspired to incorporate SMEs in these projects.

The Malaysian government recognised that among SMEs were enterprises with high growth potential. However, the actual outcome of each project was determined by the stakeholders. Since China had the larger say in each project, the incorporation of local SMEs was based on cost and technology reasons. On both counts, it was difficult for Malaysian SMEs to compete with the Chinese enterprises which are more cost competitive by virtue of scale, while they are also more technologically advanced. In numerous cases, there was a need for the participation of Chinese SOEs and Malaysian GLCs to ensure these projects were implemented properly.

In a number of these cases, the issue of industrial-financial linkages appeared core, with state-backed financial institutions providing the requisite funding. Only one privately-owned bank, the Singapore based UOB, figured in these case studies, working with privately-owned D&Y Textile. The role of large business groups from China, as lead enterprises in these projects, indicated that private firms function as multi-national companies (MNCs) in the Malaysian economy, though with the tacit support of the Chinese state. For large listed companies, however, they have recourse to the capital and bond markets to raise the funds they require and are less dependent on bank loans, as in the case of Alibaba and MAHB.

In each case, a different set of issues predominated which dictated decision-making by the state (if it was a key figure in the project) or by the business enterprise. In the case of Proton, although a private-private venture, decision-making was clearly centred in the hands of the Malaysian state. It was, ultimately, the state that decided if Geely should emerge as a major stakeholder in Proton. It was in the interest of Geely to secure a huge equity interest in Proton as this served as an avenue for this Chinese enterprise to penetrate the Southeast Asian automobile market. Geely also benefited from having Lotus under its wing as this acquisition served to expand its portfolio of technology, complementing earlier technology acquisitions. However, the sale changed the nature of Proton as DRB-HICOM as well as the state no longer have sole say in the development of this automobile enterprise. Geely now has both equity and management control in the development of Proton. Crucially too, Geely, as the technology provider, determines Proton's future growth path, in terms of new car models, revamping the existing vendor system and its competitiveness.

There was an obvious shift of structural power as the Malaysian state has less influence in the development of Proton, which will be dictated primarily by the need to register profit and increase market share. Despite its compromised position, the state continues to play a helping hand in Proton's development due to the aspired goals of this project, that is that this automobile enterprise emerges as a leading regional player. The state's fiscal position makes it increasingly difficult to provide financial assistance to an essentially privatised car project. Meanwhile, Proton has shifted from local bank financing to financing by China's SOE banks for its expansion, due to its partnership with Geely.

In the MCKIP venture, a major industrial project, the strong hand of both states is evident, indicating a novel and mutually beneficial public-public partnership, a mechanism also to ensure implementation of key policies by the governments of China and Malaysia. The MCKIP project was executed through the active involvement of government-linked enterprises from China and Malaysia, though with private sector participation. Despite the facilitating hand of the state, foreign investments in the Park were primarily due to the role played by the Chinese partner. This reflected a shift in structural power, as the Malaysian state had less influence about the types of investments that flowed into the Park. This led to a preponderance of investments in sectors China was keen to transplant abroad. While the emphasis of the Malaysian state was on nurturing production networks, comprising large firms from China and local SMEs, there is little evidence that this occurred. After all, Alliance Steel would acquire products from local SMEs only if they met its cost and technology specifications. As it stands, domestic linkages are weak and technology transfer is confined to training.

Notably too, the investment outcomes in MCKIP did not pan out as expected by the Malaysian government. The Malaysian state envisaged a park that was open to investors from all countries, not one concentrated on investments from China. This outcome was because IJM depended on its Chinese partner to bring in the investors. IJM did not have the networks to do this, as it is, after all, primarily involved in real estate, construction and plantations, not in manufacturing. In industry, IJM's only venture is the manufacture of concrete products, which is linked with its core business, construction. The lesson here is that the idea of engaging an SOE and a GLC in a joint-venture is only meaningful if they have the same sectoral interest.

The focus on regional development, with the ECER's objective of industrialising the under-developed state of Pahang by promoting inbound investments, including through MCKIP, suggests a strong policy dimension. Despite having in place a well-structured institutional architecture to fulfil these goals, the desire to drive synergistic development between the Park and Kuantan Port led, again, to a dependence on Beibu to seek out potential investors from its networks in China due to its vested interest as co-owner of the two projects. The state played a helping hand by providing the requisite infrastructure to support the development of the Park and Port.

In the DFTZ project, a distinct difference is noted in the SBR form. Although a prominent publicly-listed Malaysian GLC, MAHB, is a key figure in the DFTZ, the lead player in this project is Jack Ma's Alibaba, whose enterprise has the technological know-how and logistics networks sought by the Malaysian government. Another important reason for the DFTZ project is that the Malaysian government views it as a mechanism to nurture the domestic and export capacity of SMEs by employing an e-commerce platform. In this project, although the nature of this state-private venture is one where Alibaba was sought after, given its prominence in e-commerce, the helping hand of the state was crucial in order to provide the infrastructure to execute the project. Interestingly, the funding required for the project appears to be provided by Alibaba and MAHB, with little indication of state-backed banking enterprises offering financial support. MAHB's role, as a GLC, appears primarily to smoothen the processes involved to implement the project, by obtaining the necessary regulatory approvals as well as procuring the large land base required to create this tech platform. Investments in the DFTZ will be aligned to the e-commerce and logistics-based interests of Alibaba and Cainiao. Despite this being aligned to national interests, technology transfer and spillovers will be based on domestic capabilities, technology and costs. Although institutional complementarity is evident from the two co-owners of the project, this state-directed project, as in the case of MCKIP, is profit-driven. And, ultimately, MAHB and Alibaba have to answer to their shareholders on the profitability of the DFTZ project.

In the case of Jinko, a privately-owned enterprise from China working alone in Malaysia, what is particularly significant is that of an institutional architecture comprising federal and state-level-based institutions, collaborating in a helping hand manner to draw in this investment in the solar energy sector, an industry the government is keen to cultivate. The Penang state government and MIDA, the primary federal institution responsible for seeking out and approving foreign investments, had worked to provide the necessary incentives, as well as reduce bureaucratic red-tape, to allow Jinko to commence operations in Penang, indicating the active endeavour by the government to secure investments in a sector it is keen to promote.[1] Equally significant is that funding for Jinko's operations in Malaysia was obtained from a GLC-based financial institution, Malayan Banking, indicating that spillovers can be cross sectoral.

D&Y Textile, though another privately-owned enterprise, has its roots in the state sector. This enterprise secured funding from China for its venture in Malaysia, suggesting strong state support based on the 'going out' policy. Moreover, a review of the history of D&Y Textile indicates that this enterprise has had close ties with China's SOEs, suggesting the importance of political ties by private firms when deciding to venture abroad. As Table 4.1 indicates, there is some evidence of D&Y Textile securing funds from United Overseas Bank (UOB), a Singapore-incorporated enterprise with a branch in Malaysia. This attempt by this private firm from China to obtain loans from other sources of funds suggests an effort to attain some independence from the Chinese state. Furthermore, D&Y Textile's choice of Malaysia as its production base was due to the lower cost of raw materials and energy here, compared to China. Noteworthy too is D&Y Textile's location, in the highly industrialised state of Johor which provides first world infrastructure, including ports to facilitate the export of its products. As for the Malaysian government, with D&Y Textile's presence in the peninsula, there is an expectation of the creation of production networks, a mechanism to upgrade the skills of domestic SMEs in the textile sector. Indeed, D&Y Textile is expected to anchor a high-tech textile industrial park, though the helping hand it has secured for its Malaysian venture has come primarily from the Chinese state.

Since CRRC ZELC is a prominent SOE from China,[2] it does not appear to have problems financing its ventures, even though this enterprise is involved in a heavy industry sub-sector, the production and

---

[1] A comparison of the investment promotion in the case of Jinko and MCKIP suggests that it is much more targeted when it involves the federal bureaucratic institution, MIDA, rather than when it is left to a GLCs such as IJM.

[2] The case study notes that CRRC ZELC can be classified as a major subsidiary of a 'yang qi', that is a core group of central enterprises in China. This indicates, in China, as in Malaysia, there are different types or levels of SOEs, i.e. central and provincial enterprises. This further suggests that the state of China has an institutional architecture comprising SOEs to facilitate implementation of its development policies, in the country as well as abroad. This study, however, deals solely with the way China's SOEs—and privately-owned enterprises—function in a foreign setting, where state-state ties have been created to allow for the flow of investments into key sectors of the Southeast Asian economy.

maintenance of railway equipment. Industrial-financial links comprising SOEs clearly expedited the development of major projects in a heavy industry sector, while enabling the construction of high-priced infrastructure projects. This case study highlights that CRRC ZELC's ventures in Malaysia, including in a light rail transit (LRT) project, were awarded to it through direct negotiations with the Malaysian government, evidence of state-state ties that exhibit a grabbing hand tendency. A service and maintenance contract for another LRT line that CRRC ZELC secured through direct negotiation further indicates these strong state-state links. However, CRRC ZELC's railway production plant in Perak indicates a productive dimension to its business, with the Malaysian government exhibiting a helping hand approach to draw investments in a region in the peninsula in need of investments in the industrial sector.

Alliance Steel constitutes a case of an enterprise with an equity interest in it by a provincial government as well as a privately-owned firm from China. In this state-private venture, there is no equity participation by GLCs or privately-owned firms from Malaysia, probably because of the need to protect knowledge of production methods in this highly-competitive heavy industry enterprise. Since Alliance Steel is in an industry that requires an enormous volume of financial investment in its plant and machinery, there is ample evidence of funding support for it from financial-based SOEs, i.e. China Construction Bank, Export-Import Bank and the Agricultural Bank of China. If federal and state governments in Malaysia were active in drawing investments from Jinko, it is obvious that the government of China was a prime mover in aiding Alliance Steel's venture into Malaysia.

Interestingly too, Alliance Steel is a major occupant of land in the MCKIP industrial area, another indication of the Malaysian government's helping hand. An institutional framework comprising the governments of Malaysia and China to develop the MCKIP project appeared to be the reason why Alliance Steel's massive venture in the steel sub-sector was supported by financial-based SOEs. In Alliance Steel's operations in the MCKIP, there was little evidence by the end of 2019 to suggest that Malaysian enterprises, including SMEs, were benefiting from this investment. The preferential treatment accorded to Alliance Steel was also seen when the company was allowed by the Malaysian government to use construction supplies from China. The primary objective of the Alliance Steel venture, from the perspective of the Malaysian government, is to develop a production network involving domestic SMEs. As for the

Chinese government, by situating this enterprise in Malaysia, it hoped that Alliance Steel would benefit from this Southeast Asian country's regional trade preferential policies. China also actively promotes the export of the steel production sector. Steel production is lucrative presumably due to growing demand fuelled by major construction projects in Malaysia and the rest of Southeast Asia for BRI-linked infrastructure and other projects. Surplus production capacity in China, including in this sector, further drove the need to relocate abroad the manufacturing of steel.

Institutional Architecture, Decision-Making, Investment Flows

Important lessons can be gleaned from these case studies about the institutional architecture in place in Malaysia through which investment flows from China occur. Twelve states and the federal territory of Kuala Lumpur in the Malaysian federation have projects involving SOEs or private firms from China.[3] However, the case studies provide little evidence of coordination between federal- and state-level public agencies. In all cases, there was no evidence of the establishment of deliberation councils, as well as coordination between them, to ensure transparent and effective implementation of these projects though they involved federal and state governments, as well as a foreign government. There were no deliberation councils comprising members of the federal and state bureaucracies and private sector enterprises, though the desire to include SMEs in these ventures was a core public policy. In this institutional architecture, the flow of accurate and reliable information between the government and business sector did not appear to prevail suggesting key domestic enterprises were not included in deliberations about the development of these projects. There is little evidence of mechanisms in place to ensure Chinese multinationals conform with the Malaysian government's desire that new technology-based knowledge is transferred to SMEs or of the need to create production networks or supply chains through which technology transfer can transpire.

There is also no appropriate institutional setting for effective industrial development based on federally- or state-generated public policies. There

---

[3] The sole exception is the state of Perlis. See Appendix 1 for a list of projects in Malaysia undertaken by enterprises from China.

is little evidence of targeting of specific core sectors, though there is a focus on high value-added and high-tech manufacturing and e-commerce, seen in the case of the DFTZ, Alliance Steel and CRRC ZELC. There is, however, much evidence of highly centralised political leadership at the federal level, dictating the pattern of investment flows, visibly seen under the Najib administration, though increasingly evident under the second Mahathir Mohamad-led government. A similar sense of highly centralised political leadership is obvious in some states, specifically in Penang and Johor.[4] In this highly centralised decision-making process, there is little need for reciprocity, i.e. the capacity and autonomy of a government to secure sustainable economic performance from companies in return for subsidies or other forms of public support, a requirement in SBRs where private enterprises have access to state-generated rents. In this institutional architecture, structural power is clearly with the two strong states, in Malaysia and China, with obvious subservience of private enterprises to them.

These findings indicate that a well-functioning institutional architecture does not exist within government to ensure thoughtful and careful implementation of projects, including in major industrial ventures where the state's enterprises play a significant role as joint-venture partners. The implementation mechanism needs to consider outcomes that include contribution to technology transfer, not merely to the profitability of the enterprise. Meanwhile, an invisible hand exists, seen in the case studies on private-private ties, suggesting privately-owned firms from China and Malaysia actively seek out potentially lucrative ventures, some based on incentives offered by the government. There is clear evidence of a helping hand by the state, seen in key sectors that the government is intent on developing, for example, e-commerce, as in the case study on the DFTZ. The helping hand of the state is unmistakeable in the Proton project, comprising private enterprises from both countries, as well as in the case of D&Y Textile. In the DFTZ project, the state is actively encouraging a shift towards a new economy, the digital economy, by helping SMEs to export via an e-commerce platform. The DFTZ is expected to spearhead an e-commerce hub for the region, focusing also on digital innovations that will facilitate the aspired shift from an old to a new economy. In

---

[4] This is also much evidence of this in investments in the state of Sarawak. See Fig. 1.2 as well as Appendix. There is little indication of transparency and accountability in the implementation of these state-level ventures, specifically in mega projects.

all cases, though in particular the case of the MCKIP, innovation hubs are an expected outcome, with transfer of technology and knowledge to Malaysian SMEs. Such innovation hubs have yet to emerge. These case studies thus further suggest that well implemented policies do matter and that they shape the flow of resources and technological know-how into the industrial and manufacturing sectors that can benefit domestic firms.[5]

While state-state ties, or public-public partnerships have been created, there are fundamental differences in the way they function. This is most evident in the case studies on MCKIP, Alliance Steel and CRCC ZELC, all extremely expensive and major industrial-based projects. The mode of industrial-financial linkages in these three projects differ, though there is patent state support for their implementation. These major industrial public-public partnerships indicate most cogently the political leadership provided to ensure implementation, with those in Malaysia offering the concessions and those from China occupying the investment spaces opened to them. In the case of MCKIP, DFTZ, Alliance Steel and CRRC ZELC, it is obvious that key decisions are taken at the apex of the political system, with evidence of the presence of a helping hand in all cases. There are, however, grabbing hand practices in projects associated with CRRC ZELC, in its infrastructure-based ventures. Evidently, there are few transparency and accountability mechanisms in place in this governance system. It was the pervasiveness of grabbing hand practices that brought into question the credibility of the Malaysian government under Najib's administration.[6] During Najib's term as prime minister, his government commanded little credibility in key projects with Chinese investments, though this was most distinct in infrastructure and construction projects, a factor contributing to little mutual trust between the government and the Malaysian business community. This lack of mutual trust further contributed to Najib's dependence on China for new investments in the industrial and manufacturing sectors.

These case studies thus draw attention to the centrality of politics in decision-making in state-state, state-state-private and state-private ties. Who governs in these SBRs in these different projects differ, depending

---

[5] Conceptually, these are potentially good projects for Malaysia, but implementation is left more to market forces rather than effective state intervention.

[6] See, for example, Gomez et al. (2017) and Wright and Hope (2018). Both studies draw attention to a form of SBR where GLCs played a prominent role, but with grabbing hand features that contributed to high-level corruption.

on the nature of the project and the volume of investments involved. In the case of MCKIP, DFTZ, Alliance Steel and CRRC ZELC, the federal government in Malaysia wielded decision-making powers, though its capacity to implement these projects depended heavily on state-state-based negotiations with the Chinese government. Once up and functioning, the Chinese SOEs governed these projects, as they were primary actors in these heavy industrial ventures. In spite of a regime change, after the fall of the Najib government, it appears that there has been little change in the way these projects are managed.

SBRs, Production Networks, and SME Development

The studies of DFTZ, D&Y Textile and Jinko indicate that public-private partnerships remain crucial in the industrial sector, even in the presence of public-public partnerships. While public-public-led type investments reveal different forms of state intervention in an economy, including to drive the development of modern and technologically-upgraded industries, the role of private enterprises in the growth of new ventures to speed up industrialisation as well as to nurture SMEs remains crucial. A deconstruction of these ventures, whether based on public-public partnerships or public-private partnerships comprising two or more firms indicated significant organisational diversity.

What is evident in the case studies, specifically Alliance Steel and CRRC ZELC, is the need for the state to play a role in the financing of R&D which is expensive and potentially risky in heavy industries as well as technologically-based industries, areas of investment where the private sector would fear treading into. In these cases, the financing of these enterprises was provided by SOE-based financial institutions, an indication of the commitment of the Chinese state to their investments. The case studies further indicate that Chinese enterprises had acquired technological knowledge before venturing abroad, an outcome of investments in R&D in China. The financing they secured was to ensure that the export of their factories served their purpose, that is to move abroad due to excess capacity and environmental concerns. Such investments also serve as an attempt to expand the global reach of these enterprise as well as to ensure the competitiveness and profitability of these SOEs in the global economy.

However, on the Malaysian side, even in projects of enormous magnitude, involving targeting specific sectors to foster industrialisation, as seen in the new-technology sector through government-supported projects such as the DTFZ, the implementation is left to the designated GLC. However, the GLC's objectives are not necessarily aligned to the developmental aspects of the project. The GLCs in Malaysia are more focussed on immediate needs such as generating profits. Moreover, in each of these different sorts of SBRs, there is no evidence of effective coordination between these enterprises and public institutions, including those financial-based SOEs and GLCs. An important difference can be noted here in the links between the state and its enterprises in China and Malaysia. While China appears to be able to direct its SOEs to execute the objectives of the state, the Malaysian federal and state governments are less able to direct their GLCs to pursue and execute development plans. Although China's SOEs are clearly mandated to be commercially viable, while pursuing developmental goals, Malaysia's GLCs are more focussed on generating profits, rather than pursuing long-term economic development goals.

Interestingly, in these industrial-financial links that have been created to facilitate investment flows, the key finding from the case studies is that funding of these projects was not by the multi-lateral-based AIIB, created by the Chinese government. Where industrial-financial ties have been found, the funds have been provided by policy-based financial institutions such as the Export-Import Bank of China and the China Development Bank. In a sole case, Jinko, it was noted that a Malaysian-based GLC in the financial sector, Malayan Banking, had provided its services. In only one case too, D&Y Textile, were the services of a Singapore-based bank utilised. In the MCKIP project, IJM used Malayan Banking initially to fund its purchase of land, though it later switched to a bank from China based in Malaysia due to lower interest rates. As in the case of MCKIP, China's SOEs in the banking sector have been used to finance the later development of Proton. There is no evidence that Alibaba used any of China's SOE banks to raise funds. Alibaba employed the capital market for its expansion plans.

As Fig. 1.4 indicates, approved investments in Malaysia's manufacturing sector indicates that the largest approved investments by value were in basic metal production, cogently seen in the case of Alliance Steel. The main investments in the electrical and electronics sector were in the solar sub-sector which were mainly tariff-jumping investments, as indicated in the case study of Jinko. The case studies of D&Y Textile and Proton indicate the presence of investments in textiles and automobiles respectively, although the approved investment value is much smaller. In both cases, especially Proton, with Geely in Malaysia for the long haul, there is no evidence as yet of diffusion of technology, specifically to SMEs in the automobile industry's well-established vendor-based networks. It is possible that the second round of investments between the vendors and suppliers from China may lead to some technology spillovers for the local partners. In the high-tech sector, evident in the DFTZ case, the involvement of Alibaba was constituted a means to help SMEs to export, as well as to enable Malaysia to become a regional hub for e-commerce in Southeast Asia. This remains to be seen as the ASEAN e-commerce hub is a work-in-progress, one that is scheduled be launched in the middle of 2020.

In some of these cases, there was a clear attempt to create regionally- and globally-based supply chains and production networks, though this is yet to be seen in the case of MCKIP and DFTZ. In Malaysia, these supply chains and production networks, though led by firms from China, are meant to foster the rise of entrepreneurial, technologically-competent domestic firms. In all cases, elements of hegemony by the lead enterprise abound, that is with the Chinese firm in command, regardless whether it is an SOE or a private enterprise. However, the nature of the processes of mediation by the state in Malaysia that made this system of production possible is unclear from the case studies, more so since the government was in serious need of investments from China. The role of the Malaysian state in terms of shaping these production networks is unclear, even though incentives exist for such an endeavour, including the long-standing vendor development programme. There is little evidence that the Malaysian state can dictate to Chinese SOEs and private firms that domestic SMEs should be included in the ventures they undertake. Crucially too, there is little evidence of R&D transpiring locally among the SOEs, involving also domestic firms. There is little evidence of knowledge pooling networks comprising the lead investor from China and Malaysian SMEs.

In this regard then, in the formulation of production networks, a well-structured institutional architecture to shape policy planning in projects is obviously not in place. An institutional architecture has not been created that allows both governments to shape or re-shape the way production networks and supply chains are created, facilitated through active joint coordination, an outcome expected of large-scale projects. This is particularly crucial to ensure production capacity cooperation, to enhance the export of industries and capabilities, an expected outcome of such investment flows. In the case of China, international capacity cooperation does not mean simply selling products abroad but exporting the whole industry to different countries to help them build a more complete industrial system and manufacturing capacity. The industries that form a complete industrial system, such as iron and steel, nonferrous metals, building materials, railway, electric power, chemical industry, light textile, automobile, communications, construction machinery, aerospace, shipping and marine engineering, are the key areas of China's foreign direct investments.

When production networks or domestic and global supply chains have been formed through these SBRs, their key features differ, depending whether they are state-state, state-private, state-state-private or stand-alone ventures led by SOEs or private firms from China. This suggests different institutional regimes in each venture. The strategies adopted by SOEs in each of these ventures also differ. The case studies indicate mixed outcomes from the creation of state-state, state-private and state-state-private ties, though enterprises from China have benefited most from these state-driven partnerships.

CHAPTER 5

Conclusion

Reviewing SBRs: The Role of the State

The topography of state-business relations (SBRs) has changed dramatically. A diverse range of SBRs have emerged where the location of structural power differs. This has become acutely obvious with the growing presence of China's state-owned enterprises (SOEs) in emerging economies in Southeast Asia, a region where the presence of government-linked companies (GLCs) have a huge presence, seen particularly in Malaysia, Singapore, Indonesia and Vietnam. Growing state-state ties forged by governments have proved a crucial method to find new ways of doing business. While major privately-owned companies from China are also acquiring a growing presence in Southeast Asian economics, state-state ties have led to novel forms of SBRs involving SOEs and GLCs that function to shape the evolution of key sectors of an economy. With China's growing involvement in emerging markets through its influential and extremely financially well-endowed SOEs, the state has to be singled out as a key actor in Southeast Asian economies. China has become even more influential in Southeast Asia with its forging of state-state ties with countries in this region, a core method to expedite investment flows across the region.

Since the key firms involved in these Southeast Asian economies are SOEs or GLCs, with two governments authorising investments and executing projects through them, public-private partnerships can no longer be viewed as the sole crucial dimension of state-business ties.

In the new SBR forms that have emerged, investment decision-making patterns differ because, in these joint-ventures, governments dictate where to invest, creating too, when necessary, the policy incentives to incorporate SMEs in production networks, a core dimension of the corporate sectors of these emerging economies. Where structural power lies in these SBRs is with the state, though primarily with China dictating the mode of investment flows.

Malaysia provides an intriguing case as it has accommodated different SBRs, dictated by hegemonic state actors. This study is the first attempt to quantify and assess SBRs with growing state-state ties, where SOEs and GLCs implement policies and shape development agendas. In this context, the case studies reveal diverse and dynamic SBR forms. A heterogeneity of SOEs and private firms from China co-exist and function in tandem with each other, along with GLCs, large privately-owned enterprises and SMEs from Malaysia. The data from this study further indicates that China's SOEs operate in a diverse range of sectors, including in infrastructure development, in industrial parks, in ports and in services. The case studies indicate the presence of productive investments in the industrial sector, with a focus on manufacturing and services, which is often neglected in discussions of the BRI in Malaysia or Southeast Asia.

Clearly too, while the state under Najib Razak was in need of investments from China, there was an appreciation by bureaucrats that modes of development had to change, with industrial progress led by the state and the enterprises it owned, including those in the financial sector. State-state ties leading to novel forms of SBRs indicate that none of the existing business system typologies adequately reflect the institutional variations visible in China-linked projects. Indeed, state-state ties have resulted in the involvement of privately-owned companies in major projects. Meanwhile, private firms from China are also acting independently or with privately-owned Malaysian companies in the manufacturing and services sectors, indicating a diversity in forms of investment outcomes.

Through case studies of investments in Malaysia by enterprises from China, this volume draws clear attention to novel forms of statecraft which indicate the need to reconsider how SBRs are formulated, specifically in situations where enterprises owned by governments are active actors in domestic and foreign economies. There is evidence here of a re-conception of capitalist relations, with the presence of two highly interventionist states that deploy their leading business-based institutions as well as transnational-based public policies, such as the BRI, to achieve their goals. The inter-related themes of governance, finance and economic and enterprise development loom large in this study of SOEs and GLCs in newly-forged SBRs that are re-shaping investment flows across borders and in new economic sectors. These states, i.e. the one providing investments and those receiving them, meanwhile, have multiple aims that they are actively pursuing, such as nurturing innovation to promote technological development and cultivating entrepreneurial enterprises, including SMEs, with export capacity. Support for technology transfer was seen in the Malaysian government's attempt to create production networks involving its SMEs and multinational enterprises from China. However, investments in R&D by China's enterprises, whether SOEs or private firms, have not been as profound or deep as expected, while technology spillovers into SMEs in different manufacturing and services sub-sectors remain to be seen.

NEW SBRs, NEW IMPLICATIONS

With clear evidence now of different SBRs at play, an important issue must be noted. Within and between different SBRs, the economic and business outcomes differ, as do their implications. These SBRs can no longer be seen solely as that of an autonomous government working with independent private enterprises. In each case study, the institutional architecture within which the project was developed varied, including if industrial-financial links are created to support the venture. One major finding in this study is that only one private bank, United Overseas Bank (UOB) of Singapore, figures in industrial-financial links in these seven projects. The key banks in these industrial projects are government-owned, with a majority of these enterprises securing funds from China's SOE-based financial institutions.

There is evident institutional diversity in the nature of the relationship between politicians, bureaucrats and capitalists (foreign and domestic). Where structural power was located differed in each project, though, interestingly enough, the presence of the state's helping hand was evident in each project, with provision of funding by the developmental-type financial institutions playing a key role.

In every type of SBR identified in this study, the mode of negotiations between key actors in these two governments differed, with outcomes based also on forms of power relationship and level of state cohesiveness within its institutional architecture. In some cases, such as the DFTZ project, a private firm, Alibaba, still held the power to determine whether to invest, though a GLC was involved in the joint-venture to facilitate the entry of this Chinese enterprise in the Malaysian economy. Similarly, in the Proton project, a private-private venture, privately-owned Geely was the dominant force, dictating the reconfiguration of Malaysia's national car enterprise. In the MCKIP venture, two governments jointly decided investment patterns, though it was evident that the SOEs from China were the hegemonic force. The Malaysian government could, however, decide on the local joint-venture partners for the MCKIP project. This diversity in forms of SBRs has to be scrutinised as it informs how projects are conceived and implemented, though it is evident that the government of China, through funding by its financial institutions, is the dominant force in ultimately deciding patterns of investment.

Contributing to the complex and different modes of SBRs is that how they function varies from sector to sector. Intricate power relations abound, with different government leaders dictating the agenda through SOEs and GLCs, depending on where the project is located and who has control of these state-based business institutions. In the Malaysian federation, the leaders of the thirteen state governments have also actively cultivated investments from China. Situating where structural power lies when different state-level governments forge ties with Chinese SOEs can be difficult. Another core factor is the agenda of the politicians in power, specifically if the SBR is employed to achieve economic or political goals.

These issues merit serious consideration in each project because the case studies have indicated that although state leaders from China and Malaysia want projects completed efficiently, as this will facilitate trade and investment flows, the choice of private investors as co-partners has raised questions about transparency and accountability. In land reclamation-based projects and the construction of dams, serious concerns have emerged about the damage they have done to ecosystems, drawing attention to the grabbing hand tendencies of a strong state.[1] However, in the manufacturing and services sectors, there is a more equal power relationship between governments and private businesses, with mutual benefit, as well as an aspired development of SMEs. There is much desire to get firms

---

[1] The repercussions of mega infrastructure projects on the environment were stressed by opposition parties during Malaysia's general election in 2018, a factor that contributed to the fall of the long-ruling Barisan Nasional (see Gomez and Mohamed Nawab 2020).

to function proficiently as this generates employment, promotes industrial development and creates new products and services leading to the registering of profits.

One reason for these tripartite ties involving GLCs, SOEs and private firms is that the two states have selectively promoted them to conform with the dictates of the 'going out' and BRI policies, while simultaneously fostering development in Malaysia. An outcome of this range of goals to be achieved is that it has contributed to state-led business ties involving SOEs and GLCs, though not involving as many large and small Malaysian firms as expected. New state-business alliances inform how state-generated rents are being created and distributed, suggesting also new processes of capital accumulation and investment inputs. The implications of these different forms of state-business linkages are serious as they can go either way, that is while some are programmatically driven to foster economic growth, others may be predatory in nature serving the interests of powerful political and business elites. In many cases, both predatory and programmatic modes of development may be simultaneously occurring.

The literature draws attention to the relatively poor presence of Southeast Asian SOEs in manufacturing, an issue that raises questions about the capacity of the state to cultivate large and competitive enterprises in this sector. Since GLCs have a small presence in the manufacturing sector, the Malaysian government has cultivated Chinese SOEs to encourage industrial development. These China-based SOEs have shown a willingness to forge joint-ventures with GLCs as well as private firms in the industrial sector. With the involvement of Chinese SOEs in joint-ventures, the Malaysian government hopes to advance industrialisation, while also developing domestic entrepreneurial capacity.

State-state ties here suggest they can enhance domestic SME development, with beneficial outcomes such as increasing the purchase of local supplies, upgrading SME management skills, transferring technology facilitating SME access to capital and markets, and assisting domestic SMEs to internationalise their business. There is, however, no evidence as yet, that well-organised manufacturing-based production networks have been created, to improve labour productivity and enhance the quality of goods produced. There is also little evidence that the host state can dictate to Chinese SOEs and private firms that Malaysian SMEs must be incorporated in the ventures they undertake. Equally troubling is the limited evidence of R&D transpiring locally among the SOEs, involving domestic firms. These newly-forged SBRs do not appear to inspire key economic and market-complementing functions such as standard setting and quality upgrading.

Why these public-public partnerships appear to have worked so far is due to the presence of a diversified and active SOE sector from China, one with adequate access to funding. The viability of these SBRs is due to a strong peak in its institutional architecture, with the Chinese state in charge of dictating and directing investment flows. However, for state-state directed SBRs to function well, the state in the host economy must fulfil key conditions: their governance system must be transparent, inspire credibility, and have in place a system of reciprocity where the government indicates a willingness to ensure businesses perform in return for the support they obtain. Since there is little evidence of all three conditions in Malaysia, major reforms are required while state capabilities must improve.

Crucially too, policy coherence is imperative in a situation of much state-state ties that direct how companies are to function in an economy. There is little evidence of this in Malaysia, though China's development agenda, such as the BRI, comes across as a well-conceived plan, with this government also showing the capacity to respond quickly to institute changes when they are required. In Malaysia, in order to have well-conceived policies, there is clear evidence that institutional reforms, specifically to link relevant developmental and finance-based agencies, are essential. These institutional reforms are also crucial in order to create a well-functioning public delivery system, to ensure effective implementation of projects and good employment of foreign and domestic investments.

State-state ties can prove beneficial to emerging economies as China is becoming more selective with its foreign investments. Moreover, state-state ties can facilitate as well as hasten investment flows into crucial sectors of an emerging economy. The short-term outcomes of the investments under review suggest that state-state-led SBRs can be effective, with the right institutional framework and a well-conceived industrial policy. This system can promote authoritative policy-driven allocations that foster new industries and enhance SME development, though there is little evidence of this in the case studies. By helping create SOE-SME production networks and supply chains, these links can build firm capabilities, foster knowledge spillovers and encourage technological upgrading.

In emerging Southeast Asia, a clear concern is that a well-constructed institutional architecture is not in place, one that can shape investment flows through a well-defined and appropriate institutional setting to ensure effective industrial development based on well-outlined policies. This appears to be a problem in Malaysia, possibly also in the Indo-China countries, as well as in Indonesia and the Philippines.[2] The need for such an institutional architecture by Southeast Asian governments is imperative as a major shift in structural power has occurred in SBRs with decision-making authority now primarily with the large MNC-type Chinese SOEs. A core reason for this shift is that China has extraordinary outreach and a potentially huge impact on developing economies by funding major projects, implemented by SOEs with technological know-how to deliver results of high value. Importantly too, through these public-public partnerships, Chinese SOEs gain entry into numerous key sectors in developing economies. Without a well-defined institutional architecture to ensure that these investments flow into priority sectors in these Southeast Asian economies, this can lead to sub-optimal structural transformation or the exploitation of resources and new inequitable patterns of development.

---

[2] This contention is based on research undertaken in Indonesia and the Philippines. For the case of the Philippines, an article has been prepared, tentatively entitled 'Strongmen Politics and Investment Flows: China's Investments in the Philippines and Malaysia'.

Appendix 1: Investments by Firms from China in Malaysia

Projects by Form of Ownership (1): State-State

Project Name	Partners (MY State)	Partners (CHN State)
Federal Level		
East Coast Rail Link (ECRL)	Malaysia Rail Link Sdn Bhd	China Communications Construction Company (CCCC)
Malaysia-China Kuantan Industrial Park & Kuantan Port (MCKIP)	Kuantan Pahang Holding (PSK/PKNP 30%, IJM 40%, Sime Darby Property 30%)	Guangxi Beibu Gulf International Port group, Qinzhou Investment Development Co. Ltd
Kuantan Port Expansion (New Deep-Water Terminal)	IJM Corp Bhd	Guangxi Beibu International Port Group
Sarawak Bakun Dam	Sarawak Hidro Sdn Bhd, Sime Darby Bhd, Muhibbah Engineering (part of IMPSA consortium)	Sinohydro Corporation
Tun Razak Exchange (TRX)	TRX City Sdn Bhd, Gadang Holdings Bhd	China Railway First Group
Exchange 106, signature tower in TRX City	Mulia Group	China State Construction Engineering
Projects in KL Eco City	SP Setia	China Construction Development
Penang Second Bridge	UEM Builders, Jambatan Kedua Sdn Bhd	China Harbour & Engineering Corporation

(continued)

(continued)

Project Name	Partners (MY State)	Partners (CHN State)
Cement clinker production line	Negeri Sembilan Cement Industries	Sinoma International (and its Malaysian subsidiary)
Automated storage and retrieval system for Pengerang Integrated Complex	Petronas Refinery and Petrochemical Corporation Sdn Bhd	Sinopec Engineering Group
Olefins storage units in Pengerang Integrated Complex	Petronas Refinery and Petrochemical Corporation Sdn Bhd	China Petroleum Pipeline Bureau
Collaboration between Bursa Malaysia and Shanghai Stock Exchange	Bursa Malaysia	Shanghai Stock Exchange
State-Level		
Upgrading and repair of water treatment and distribution facilities in Kemaman	Terengganu State Government	Beijing Enterprises Water Group
Robotic Future City	Johor Corp	Siasun Robot & Automation Co. Ltd, under the Chinese Academy of Sciences

Projects by Form of Ownership (2): State-Private

Project Name	Partners (MY State)	Partners (MY Private)	Partners (CHN State)	Partners (CHN Private)
Federal Level				
KLIA Aeropolis DFTZ Park—Electronic World Trade Platform Initiative	Malaysia Airports Holdings Bhd	None	None	Alibaba Group Holding—Cainiao Network
1mil KW Coal-Fired Power plant project in Manjung	TNB Janamanjung Sdn Bhd	None	China National Machinery Import & Export Corporation	Alstom (subsidiary in China)

(continued)

(continued)

Project Name	Partners (MY State)	Partners (MY Private)	Partners (CHN State)	Partners (CHN Private)
Bird's Nest Research and Development Collaboration	Universiti Putra Malaysia	Royal Bird's Nest Sdn Bhd, Universiti Tunku Abdul Rahman	Peking University	None
MMU-ZTE Training Centre for technological innovation & vocational coaching	Multimedia University (MMU)	None	None	ZTE
Celcom LTE Network Upgrade	Celcom Axiata Bhd	Ericsson Malaysia Sdn Bhd	None	Huawei Technologies
State Level				
Baleh hydroelectric dam project's civil works, Sarawak	Sarawak Energy Bhd	Untang Jaya Sdn Bhd	Gezhouba Engineering	None
Kedah Integrated Fishery Terminal	Kedah Government	None	None	Lu Hai Feng Ltd
Paradiso Nuova	Medini Iskandar Malaysia	None	None	Zhuoda Group
Forest City	Esplanade Danga 88 Sdn Bhd	None	None	Country Garden Group
Methanol and methanol derivatives project in Sarawak	Yayasan Hartanah Bumiputera Sarawak (YHBS)	MacFeam	Huanqiu Contracting and Engineering (HQC)	None

MY Private with CHN State

Project Name	Partners (MY Private)	Partners (CHN State)
Penang Port (revamping projects)	KAJ Development Sdn Bhd	Shenzhen Yantian Port Group Co. Ltd, Rizho Port Group Co. Ltd
Melaka Gateway	KAJ Development Sdn Bhd	PowerChina International Group Ltd
Danga Bay	Iskandar Waterfront Holdings	Hao Yuan Investments Pte Ltd
Greenland Tebrau Bay	Iskandar Waterfront Holdings	Greenland Group
Pavilion Elite & Royale Pavilion Hotel	Malton Group, Urusharta Cemerlang (KL)	Beijing Urban Construction Group (BUCG)
Pearl KLCC	Malton Group	Beijing Urban Construction Group (BUCG)
3rdNvenue	Titijaya Land Bhd	CREC Development (M) Sdn Bhd
The Shore	Titijaya Land Bhd	CREC Development (M) Sdn Bhd
M101 Skywheel	M101 Holdings Sdn Bhd	China Railway Construction Corporation (CRCC)
Paragon @ KL Northgate	Anzo Holdings	MCC Overseas
Development Land at Jalan Raja Chulan	City Centre Sdn Bhd	China Vanke Co. Ltd
Seremban 2	Paramount Blossom	China Railway Liuyuan Group
Seri Tanjung Pinang—Waterfront Land Reclamation	Tanjung Pinang Development Sdn Bhd	China Communications Construction Company (CCCC)
Kuantan Waterfront Resort City	Puri Holdings Bhd	CCCC Dredging Group Ltd Bina
Construction of Halal Vaccine and Pharmaceutical Plant (Negeri Sembilan)	GB Asiatic Ventures Sdn Bhd	China Machinery Engineering Corporation (CMEC)
HELP International School	HELP Group	Beijing Urban Construction Group (BUCG)
Infrastructure for National Defence Education Centre (Puspahanas) in Putrajaya—Phase 1	Awan Megah Sdn Bhd	China Road & Bridge Corporation

(continued)

(continued)

Project Name	Partners (MY Private)	Partners (CHN State)
Green Technology Park in Pekan, Pahang (Phases 2 & 3)	Nextgreen Global Bhd	China Nuclear Industry Huaxing Construction Co. Ltd
Gemas Johor Electrified Double Tracking Rail	YTL Corp Bhd, Fajarbaru Builders Sdn Bhd, SIPP Railway Sdn Bhd	China Railway Construction Corp Ltd (CRCC), China Railway Engineering Corp (CREC) & China Communications Construction Corp (CCCC)
Kulai Linggi International Port (KLIP)	Linggi Base Sdn Bhd	China Railway Port Channel Engineering Group Co. Ltd
MRT Line 2 Sungai Buloh—Serdang—Putrajaya	George Kent (Malaysia) Bhd	China Communications Construction Co. Ltd
Penang Undersea Tunnel	Zenith Construction, Vertice Bhd, Juteras Sdn Bhd, Kenanga Nominees (Tempatan) Sdn Bhd	China Railway Construction Corp, previously included BUCG
Combined-cycle gas turbine power plant project in Sabah	Ranhill Holdings Bhd	China National Electric Equipment Corp
Laying of fibre optic submarine cable between Kuching and Singapore	PP Telecom	Wuhan Fiberhome International
Steel Mill in Terengganu	Hiap Teck Venture Bhd	China Shougang Group
LRT3 (Light Rail Vehicle Package)	Tegap Dinamik Sdn Bhd	CRRC Zhuzhou Locomotive Co. Ltd (with Siemens Ltd China)
Modification of coal system at YTL Perak-Hanjoong cement plant	YTL Cement	Sinoma International Engineering

Projects by Form of Ownership (3): Private-Private

Project Name	Partners (MY Private)	Partners (CHN Private)
Redevelopment of Plaza Rakyat	Gabungan Tiasa Sdn Bhd	Debao Property Development Ltd

(continued)

(continued)

Project Name	Partners (MY Private)	Partners (CHN Private)
Country Garden Diamond City	Mayland Group	Country Garden Holdings
Serendah Project	Mayland Group	Country Garden Holdings
Central Park at Tampoi	Damansara Realty Bhd	Country Garden Holdings
Impression City Melaka	Yong Tai Bhd	China Impression Wonders Arts Development Co. Ltd Funding: Sino Haijing Holdings Ltd
Agile Mont Kiara	PJ Development Holdings Bhd	Agile Real Estate Development (M) Sdn Bhd
The Haven Lakeside Residences, Ipoh	Bina Puri Holdings Bhd	Beijing Construction Engineering Group International (Malaysia) Sdn Bhd
Wood Pulp Mill in Sabah	Pandawa Sakti Sdn Bhd	China CEC Engineering Corporation
Precast concrete panel manufacturing plant in Nilai	MGB	Sany Construction Industry Development
Geely-Proton-Lotus	DRB Hicom	Geely Holding
Alipay mobile wallet services	Maybank, Touch N' Go	Alibaba Group - Ant Financial Services Group
Development of 5G mobile network technologies	U Mobile Sdn Bhd	ZTE
Banana growing and trading	Dashang Group	

Projects by Form of Ownership (4): Chinese firms only

Project Name	Partners (CHN State)	Partners (CHN Private)
Kuala Ketil Solar PV Project	CEEC Tianjin Electronic Power, Edra Power Holdings Sdn Bhd	
Country Garden (Danga Bay)		Country Garden Holdings

(continued)

(continued)

Project Name	Partners (CHN State)	Partners (CHN Private)
Xiamen University Malaysia	Sinohydro Corporation Malaysia, Xiamen University	
R&F Princess Cove project (Tanjung Puteri)		Guangzhou R&F Properties
Greenland Jade Palace (Danga Bay)	Greenland Group	
The M-Macrolink Medini (Iskandar Puteri)		Macrolink Group
Greenfield Residence (Bandar Sunway		CICET Asia Development Sdn Bhd
Lake Point Residence (Cyberjaya)		Yanjian Group
3.5 million tonne capacity steel mill in Pahang	Guangxi Beibu Gulf International Port Group	
Aluminum component manufacturing (MCKIP)	Guangxi Investment Group	
Samalaju Industrial Park Steel Complex	MCC Overseas	Hebei Xinwuan Steel Group
Manufacturing of renewable energy applications (MCKIP)		Zkenergy (yiyang) New Resources Science & Technology Co. Ltd
Crystalline silicon solar cells and modules production (MCKIP)		Wuxi Suntech
Manufacturing of PV Cells and Modules in Bayan Lepas	Jinko Solar Technology Sdn Bhd	
Manufacturing of Solar and PV Panels in Batu Kawan		JA Solar Malaysia Sdn Bhd
Manufacturing of photovoltaic functional glass in Melaka		Xinyi Solar (Malaysia) Sdn Bhd
Manufacturing of solar ingots and wafer slicing in Sarawak		Comtec Solar Systems Group Ltd
Integrated manufacturing facility of solar ingot, water cells and modules in Sarawak		Longi (Kuching) Sdn Bhd
Manufacturing of bio-stimulant for soil reconditioning in Pahang		Beijing Goldenway Biology Tech Co Ltd
Expansion of heavy machinery factories in Dengkil and Sepang		CIH Malaysia
Rolling stock manufacturing and maintenance base in Perak	CRRC Rolling Stock Center Sdn Bhd	

(continued)

(continued)

Project Name	Partners (CHN State)	Partners (CHN Private)
Clay porcelain manufacturing in Kuantan		Guangxi Zhongli Enterprise Group Co Ltd Group Co
Tyre Factory in Selangor	Qingdao FullRun Tyre Corp Ltd	
Glass production		Kibing Group
Glass panel manufacturing plant		Xinyi Glass
Textile factory in Johor		D&Y Textile Group
Acquisition of 51% equity stake in Shell Refining Company	Malaysia Hengyuan International Ltd	
Acquisition of assets of Edra Global Energy Bhd	China General Nuclear Power Corporation (CGN)	

Source Compiled by authors, as at 31 December 2019

Bibliography

Amable, B. 2003. *The Diversity of Modern Capitalism*. Oxford: Oxford University Press.

Barber, B. 2018. Authoritarianism Gains in Southeast Asia. *The Foreign Service Journal*, May. https://www.afsa.org/authoritarianism-gains-southeast-asia.

Buur, L. and Whitfield, L. 2013. Industrial Policy and State-Business Relations: Towards a Heuristic Approach. In D.W. te Velde (ed.), *State-Business Relations and Industrial Policy: Current Policy and Research Debates*. London: ESRC DFID Growth Research Programme.

Chang, Y.-Y. 2019. Understanding the Belt and Road Initiative (BRI): An Initiative to Make China Great Again? *European Journal of East Asian Studies*, 18: 7–35.

Chen, Y.A., Wang, X.J. and Young, M. 2015. Geely's Acquisition of Volvo. *Asian Case Research Journal*, 19 (1): 183–202.

Cheong, K.C and Yong, C.C. 2019. Assessing ASEAN's Relevance: Have the Right Questions Been Asked? *Journal of Southeast Asian Economies*, 36 (1): 11–24.

Culpepper, P. 2010. *Quiet Politics and Business Power: Corporate Control in Europe and Japan*. Cambridge: Cambridge University Press.

Culpepper, P. 2015. Structural Power and Political Science in the Post-crisis Era. *Business and Politics*, 17 (3): 391–409.

Department of Statistics (DOS) Malaysia (various years). Statistics on Foreign Direct Investment in Malaysia. https://www.dosm.gov.my/.

de Graaff, N. and B. van Apeldoorn. 2018. US-China Relations and the Liberal World Order: Contending Elites, Colliding Visions? *International Affairs*, 94 (1): 113–131.

Economic Planning Unit (EPU) and World Bank. 2011. *Moving Up the Value Chain: A Study of Malaysia's Solar and Medical Device Industries*. Washington, DC: World Bank.

Farrell, H. and Newman, A.L. 2015. Structuring Power: Business and Authority Beyond the Nation State. *Business and Politics*, 17 (3): 527–552.

Frankopan, P. 2018. *The New Silk Roads: The Present and Future of the World*. London: Bloomsbury.

Frye, T. and Shleifer, A. 1997. The Invisible Hand and the Grabbing Hand. *The American Economic Review*, 87 (2): 354–358.

Fuchs, D. and Lederer, M. 2007. The Power of Business. *Business and Politics*, 9 (3): 1–17.

Gomez, E.T. 2012. The Politics and Policies of Corporate Development: Race, Rents and Redistribution in Malaysia. In H. Hill, S.Y. Tham and M.Z. Ragayah (eds), *Malaysia's Development Challenges: Graduating from the Middle*. London: Routledge: 63–82.

Gomez, E.T. and Lafaye de Micheaux, E. 2017. Diversity of Southeast Asian Capitalisms: Evolving State-Business Relations in Malaysia. *Journal of Contemporary Asia*, 47 (5): 792–814.

Gomez, E.T. and Mohamed Nawab, M.O. (eds). 2020. *Malaysia's 14th General Election and UMNO's Fall: Intra-Elite Feuding and the Pursuit of Power*. London: Routledge.

Gomez, E.T., Fikri, F., Padmanabhan, T. and Juwairiah, T. 2018. *Governments in Business: Diverse Forms of Intervention*. Kuala Lumpur: Institute for Democracy & Economic Affairs (IDEAS).

Gomez, E.T., Padmanabhan, T., Norfaryanti, K., Bhalla, S. and Fikri, F. 2017. *Minister of Finance Incorporated: Ownership and Control of Corporate Malaysia*. Singapore: Palgrave Macmillan.

Hall, P. and Soskice, D. (eds). 2001. *Varieties of Capitalism*. New York: Oxford University Press.

Holcombe, R.G. 2018. *Political Capitalism: How Economic and Political Power Is Made and Maintained*. Cambridge: Cambridge University Press.

Jomo K.S. 1994. The Proton Saga: Malaysian Car, Mitsubishi Gain. In K.S. Jomo (ed.), *Japan and Malaysian Development: In the Shadow of the Rising Sun*. London: Routledge: 263–290.

Kang, C., Hillman, A.L. and Gu, Q-Y. 2002. From the Helping Hand to the Grabbing Hand: Fiscal Federalism and Corruption in China. In J. Wong and D. Lu (eds.), *China's Economy into the New Century*. Singapore: World Scientific: 193–215.

Khanna, T. and Yafeh, Y. 2007. Business Groups in Emerging Markets: Paragons or Parasites? *Journal of Economic Literature*, 45 (2): 331–372.

Khor Y.L. 2013. The Significance of China-Malaysia Industrial Parks. *ISEAS Perspective*, 17 June. Singapore: ISEAS.

Koo, A.Y.C. 1990. The Contract Responsibility System: Transition from a Planned to a Market Economy. Economic Development and Cultural Change, 38 (4): 797–820.

Kurlantzick, J. 2018. Southeast Asia's Populism is Different But also Dangerous. Council of Foreign Relations, 1 November. https://www.cfr.org/in-brief/southeast-asias-populism-different-also-dangerous.

Leftwich, A. 2008. *States of Development: On the Primacy of Politics in Development*. Cambridge: Polity Press.

Leonard, J.L. 1980. Review: Multinational Corporations and Politics in Developing Countries. *World Politics*, 32 (3): 454–483.

Li, R. and Cheong, K.C. 2019. *China's State Enterprises: Changing Role in a Rapidly Transforming Economy*. Singapore: Palgrave Macmillan.

Li, Y. 2018. China's Go Out Policy—A Review on China's Promotion Policy for Outward Foreign Direct Investment from a Historical Perspective. IWE Working Papers 244, Institute for World Economics—Centre for Economic and Regional Studies, Hungarian Academy of Sciences.

Lund, S., Manyika, J., Woetzel, J., Bughin, J., Krishnan, M., Seong, J. and Muir, M. 2019. *Globalization in Transition: The Future of Trade and Value Chains*. Washington, DC: McKinsey Global Institute.

Malaysian Industry Government Group for High Technology (MIGHT) 2015. *Malaysian Aerospace Industry Blueprint 2030*. Kuala Lumpur: MIGHT.

Maxfield, S. and Schneider, B.R. 1997. *Business and the State in Developing Countries*. Ithaca: Cornell University Press.

McCarthy, S. and Thompson, M.R. (eds.). 2019. *Governance and Democracy in the Asia-Pacific: Political and Civil Society*. London: Routledge.

Miller, T. 2017. *China's Asian Dream: Empire Building Along the New Silk Road*. London: Zed Books.

Ngeow, C.B. 2019. Economic Cooperation and Infrastructure Linkage Between Malaysia and China under the Belt and Road Initiative. In F.M. Cheung and Y.Y. Hong (eds.), *Regional Connection under the Belt and Road Initiative: The Prospects for Economic and Financial Cooperation*. London: Routledge.

Olson, M. 1982. *The Rise and Decline of Nations: Economic Growth, Stagflation, and Social Rigidities*. New Haven: Yale University Press.

Pei. M. 2016. *China's Crony Capitalism: The Dynamics of Regime Decay*. Cambridge, MA: Harvard University Press.

Rodrik, D. 2004. *Industrial Policy for the Twenty-First Century*. Vienna: UNIDO.

Schneider, B.R. 2009. A Comparative Political Economy of Diversified Business Groups, or How States Organize Big Business. *Review of International Political Economy*, 16 (2): 178–201.

Sen, K. (ed.). 2013. *State-Business Relations and Economic Development in Africa and India*. London: Routledge.

Shen, R. and Mantzopoulos, V. 2013. China's "Going Out" Policy: Inception, Evolution, Implication. *Journal of Business and Behavioral Sciences*, 25 (2): 121–136.

Shleifer, A. and Vishny, R.W. 1993. Corruption. *Quarterly Journal of Economics*, 108 (3): 599–617.

Singh, J.N. and Chen, G.C. 2017. State-Owned Enterprises and the Political Economy of State-State Relations in the Developing World. *Third World Quarterly*, 39 (6): 1–21.

te Velde, D.W. (ed.) 2010. *Effective State-Business Relations, Industrial Policy and Economic Growth*. London: ODI.

Tham, S.Y., Kam, A.J.Y. and Aziz, N.I.A. 2016. Moving up the value chain in ICT: ASEAN trade with China. *Journal of Contemporary Asia*, 46 (4): 680–699.

Tham, S.Y. 2019. Malaysia and the BRI: The Case of the Kuantan Port. *ISEAS Perspective*, 15 January. Singapore: ISEAS.

Tham, S.Y. and Kam, A.J.Y. 2019. Exploring the Trade Potential of the DTZ for Malaysian SMEs. *Trends in Southeast Asia, 2019, No. 3*. Singapore: ISEAS. https://www.iseas.edu.sg/images/pdf/TRS3_19%20(002).pdf.

Tham, S.Y., Kam, A.J.Y. and Tee, B.A. 2019. US-China Trade War: Potential Trade and Investment Spill-overs into Malaysia. *Asian Economic Papers*, 18 (3): 117–141.

Thompson, M.R. 2019. *Authoritarian Modernism in East Asia*. New York: Palgrave Macmillan.

Tong, J.T. and Lim, N.C. 2012. Proton: Its Rise, Fall and Future Prospects. *Asian Case Research Journal*, 16 (2): 347–377.

UNCTAD. 2014. *Trade Remedies Targeting the Renewable Energy Sector*. Geneva: UNCTAD.

Weiss, L. and Thurbon, E. 2018. Power Paradox: How the Extension of US Infrastructural Power Abroad Diminishes State Capacity at Home. *Review of International Political Economy*, 25 (6): 779–810.

Whitley, R. 1999. *Divergent Capitalisms: The Social Structuring and Change of Business Systems*. Oxford: Oxford University Press.

Woll, C. 2008. *Firm Interests: How Governments Shape Business Lobbying*. Ithaca: Cornell University Press.

Wright, T. and Hope, B. 2018. *Billion Dollar Whale: The Man Who Fooled Wall Street, Hollywood and the World*. New York: Hachette Books.

GPSR Compliance

The European Union's (EU) General Product Safety Regulation (GPSR) is a set of rules that requires consumer products to be safe and our obligations to ensure this.

If you have any concerns about our products, you can contact us on

ProductSafety@springernature.com

In case Publisher is established outside the EU, the EU authorized representative is:

Springer Nature Customer Service Center GmbH
Europaplatz 3
69115 Heidelberg, Germany